Open Source Library Systems

LIBRARY INFORMATION TECHNOLOGY ASSOCIATION (LITA) GUIDES

The Library Information and Technology Association became part of Core: Leadership, Infrastructure, Futures, also a division of the American Library Association, in September 2020. Guides published in this series retain the series title LITA Guides.

Marta Mestrovic Deyrup, PhD
Acquisitions Editor, Core, a division of the American Library Association

The Library Information Technology Association (LITA) Guides provide information and guidance on topics related to cutting-edge technology for library and IT specialists.

Written by top professionals in the field of technology, the guides are sought after by librarians wishing to learn a new skill or to become current in today's best practices.

Each book in the series has been overseen editorially since conception by LITA and reviewed by LITA members with special expertise in the specialty area of the book.

Established in 1966 and integrated as part of Core in 2020, LITA provided its members and the library and information science community as a whole with a forum for discussion, an environment for learning, and a program for actions on the design, development, and implementation of automated and technological systems in the library and information science field.

Approximately twenty-five LITA Guides were published by Neal-Schuman and ALA between 2007 and 2015. Rowman & Littlefield and LITA published the series 2015–2021. Books in the series published by Rowman & Littlefield are:

Digitizing Flat Media: Principles and Practices
The Librarian's Introduction to Programming Languages
Library Service Design: A LITA Guide to Holistic Assessment, Insight, and Improvement
Data Visualization: A Guide to Visual Storytelling for Librarians
Mobile Technologies in Libraries: A LITA Guide
Innovative LibGuides Applications
Integrating LibGuides into Library Websites
Protecting Patron Privacy: A LITA Guide
The LITA Leadership Guide: The Librarian as Entrepreneur, Leader, and Technologist

Using Social Media to Build Library Communities: A LITA Guide
Managing Library Technology: A LITA Guide
The LITA Guide to No- or Low-Cost Technology Tools for Libraries
Big Data Shocks: An Introduction to Big Data for Librarians and Information Professionals
The Savvy Academic Librarian's Guide to Technological Innovation: Moving Beyond the Wow Factor
The LITA Guide to Augmented Reality in Libraries
Digital Curation Projects Made Easy: A Step-By-Step Guide for Libraries, Archives, and Museums
Library Technology Planning for Today and Tomorrow: A LITA Guide
Tech for All: Moving beyond the Digital Divide
Change Management for Library Technologists: A LITA Guide
Makerspace and Collaborative Technologies: A LITA Guide
Change the World Using Social Media
Information Technology for Librarians and Information Professionals
Creating Inclusive Libraries by Applying Universal Design: A Guide
Sustainable Strategies for Optimizing Digital Stewardship: A Guide for Libraries, Archives, and Museums

Open Source Library Systems

A Guide

Robert Wilson and James Mitchell

ROWMAN & LITTLEFIELD
Lanham • Boulder • New York • London

Published by Rowman & Littlefield
An imprint of The Rowman & Littlefield Publishing Group, Inc.
4501 Forbes Boulevard, Suite 200, Lanham, Maryland 20706
www.rowman.com

6 Tinworth Street, London SE11 5AL, United Kingdom

Copyright © 2021 by American Library Association

All rights reserved. No part of this book may be reproduced in any form or by any electronic or mechanical means, including information storage and retrieval systems, without written permission from the publisher, except by a reviewer who may quote passages in a review.

British Library Cataloguing in Publication Information Available

Library of Congress Cataloging-in-Publication Data
Library of Congress Cataloging-in-Publication Data
Names: Wilson, Robert, 1985- author. | Mitchell, James, 1985- author.
Title: Open source library systems : a guide / Robert Wilson and James Mitchell.
Description: Lanham : Rowman & Littlefield, [2021] | Series: LITA guides | Includes bibliographical references and index.
Identifiers: LCCN 2021018663 (print) | LCCN 2021018664 (ebook) | ISBN 9781538141380 (cloth) | ISBN 9781538141397 (paperback) | ISBN 9781538141403 (ebook)
Subjects: LCSH: Open source software--Library applications. | Libraries--Information technology. | Libraries--Automation.
Classification: LCC Z678.93.O65 W55 2021 (print) | LCC Z678.93.O65 (ebook) | DDC 005.3--dc23
LC record available at https://lccn.loc.gov/2021018663
LC ebook record available at https://lccn.loc.gov/2021018664

For Lauren
—R.W.

For Jessica, Luke, and Levi
—J.R.M.

Contents

Acknowledgments		xi
Preface		xiii
1	Open Source Software: A Reorientation	1
2	Open Source Software in Libraries	15
3	Open Source ILS	27
4	Open Source and Digital Repositories	55
5	Open Source Discovery	77
6	Open Source Resource Sharing	97
7	Open Source Electronic Resource Management	109
8	Additional Open Source Systems	121
9	Libraries, Open Source Software, and the Future	133
Appendix A Notes on Library System Implementations		139
Appendix B ILS Selection & Migration Example		143
Index		153
About the Authors		155

Acknowledgments

We would both like to thank our editor, Charles Harmon, for his assistance and invaluable feedback throughout the whole publication process. Additionally, Erinn Slanina patiently answered several questions and provided correction as two authors felt their way through the manuscript publication process for the first time. We would also like to thank the numerous interviewees who contributed their stories and the stories of their institutions to this project. In particular, we'd like to thank Sonia Bouis, Gretchen Gueguen, André Lahmann, Troy Leonard, Michael Levy, Mark Noble, Jordan Piščanc, Keely Ward, Marie Wenander, and Marie Widigson.

To the numerous others who answered questions and listened as we've talked about this project, thanks are also due.

Of course, if any faults remain in this guide, they should not be attributed to any of the aforementioned but, instead, to us.

—J.R.M. & R.W.

First of all, I would like to thank my co-author and collaborator on this project, Robert Wilson. Without his support and encouragement, my contributions to this guide would have been significantly diminished. It may never have seen the light of day without him. Additionally, I would like to thank Derek Malone of the University of North Alabama's Collier Library for supporting me in this endeavor. I would also like to thank Hunter Tinsley of Collier Library's Interlibrary Loan department. He was always so quick to acquire resources to which we didn't have immediate access. Finally, I would like to thank Jessica Mitchell, my partner in life. In so many inarticulable ways, she has supported and encouraged me each day. Not only would I not have had the opportunity to write this guide, but I certainly also would not be where I am today without her.

—James Mitchell

Sincerest thanks to James Mitchell. To get to work with someone as equally passionate about this subject and, at times, equally frustrated with the state of library systems today made this project that much more rewarding. I also must thank the talented and dedicated faculty and staff at Middle Tennessee State University's Walker Library for their support and welcoming nature since my arrival there in 2018. Additionally, many thanks must go to Marshall Breeding, as much of this guide would not be possible without Marshall's vast knowledge and bibliography on library systems and the database he maintains at libraries.org as well as the personal assistance he provided when collecting some of the data used in this guide from libraries.org. Finally, thanks to my partner, Lauren Gallina, the most talented and dedicated librarian I know. If not for her unending support, guidance, and love, none of this would have been possible.

—Robert Wilson

Preface

The idea for this book has its roots in the first time the authors met. We were both attending a regional user group meeting for a particular integrated library system (ILS) and were relative newcomers to our respective institutions. We bonded over the frustration and helplessness we felt in the face of a consolidated ILS market and what seemed to be vendors who were intent on selling a new line of products when their current products sorely needed fixes and enhancements. It seemed that at least some portion of the library software market was interested in a traditional approach that we believed the larger software industry had begun to leave behind.

From these initial conversations, we discovered a common interest in open source software and the various ways open source communities, particularly within the library ecosystem, appeared to be more responsive to the concerns of libraries. Through these conversations, we noticed that relatively little had been published on open source software in the library literature over the past decade. In that span of time, the information technology (IT) industry had changed drastically. Many of these changes had far-reaching effects for open source communities as well. As a result, this book attempts to fill the gap in the library literature by bringing the conversation up to date and presenting many of these changes in an approachable format for all library stakeholders.

In chapter 1, we offer a brief history of open source software from its origins in computer science research to today. Chapter 2 provides an overview of open source software within the history of libraries and library automation. Because of its continued importance as the primary software in libraries today, we begin by considering open source integrated library systems and library service platforms in chapter 3. Chapters 4 through 7 introduce open source digital repositories, discovery layers, resource sharing platforms, and electronic resource management software, respectively. In each of these chapters, we provide a brief history of open source software in these areas. We also provide an historical and technical overview of several of the key open source applications, along with a brief treatment of service providers, in each domain. Chapter 8 covers open source archival management systems and other open source software libraries frequently used in their day-to-day management. The final chapter, chapter 9, concludes our guide by summarizing and arguing for consideration of open source software alongside other traditional options.

To give the reader a better idea of this guide's scope, we wish to also say a word about related content we do not address in this guide.

First of all, this guide does not address free and open source *tools* librarians may use on a daily basis. Instead, the authors focus their attention on systems for the storage, preservation, and access of digital and physical assets, along with its metadata. Tools like MarcEdit, OpenRefine, and GNU command line tools, while they are important, receive little or no attention in this guide. The authors believe this would stretch the scope of this guide beyond manageable limits. For readers who are interested in a recent introduction to some of these tools, we recommend Kyle Banerjee's helpful book, *The Data Wrangler's Handbook: Simple Tools for Powerful Results*.

Additionally, this guide is not intended to serve as a project management handbook to assist librarians in the migration process. Instead, we seek to provide a preliminary introduction to the open source communities many libraries may join if they choose open source solutions. Nevertheless, in the appendices of this guide, we have provided a brief overview of the selection and implementation process for various library systems, along with a discussion of the various challenges one might face in the system implementation process. These appendices are applicable to projects regardless of whether an open source solution is under consideration or not. For those readers who are interested in a detailed treatment of the migration process, we recommend *Migrating Library Data: A Practical Manual* edited by Kyle Banerjee and Bonnie Parks.

We also do not cover open educational resources (OER) or open access (OA) as a part of this guide. While these topics are of interest to librarians, they are complex and sophisticated enough to receive treatment in their own right. Any treatment the authors would have given to OER and OA in this book would have proven inadequate. A great example of a book-length treatment of OER is the book *OER: A Field Guide for Academic Librarians* by Andrew Wesolek, Jonathan Lashley, and Anne Langley. *Open Access* by Peter Suber is also a great resource for those who are interested in getting started learning about OA. This book is available online, as one might hope, via open access. These are just a couple of the numerous resources available to the librarian who would be interested in these issues.

Finally, we wish to say something about the tone of this guide. Some portions of this guide may read as unnecessarily apologetic. Open source has permeated the IT sector to such an extent that it seems ridiculous to question or argue for its permanence. Even within the library ecosystem, the persistence of some open source systems through the years coupled with new, large-scale efforts to develop open source solutions to library operations gives the observer the impression that the future of open source is secure. While we agree that open source communities and open source software are one of the keys to the future of library technology operations, we also believe that the future is not written in stone. There are no guarantees that an alternative approach to software development won't win out because it proves to be more efficient or safeguards the interests of various stakeholders. Thus, we think it's important to remind the reader of the intangible and the practical concerns that open source options address for libraries, museums, and archives.

In writing this guide, our goal was a modest one. We have sought to provide current and future librarians with an introduction to the open source ecosystem and encourage them to keep an open mind when it comes to open source software. Whether we have succeeded in this endeavor or not will be up to you, the reader.

1

Open Source Software

A Reorientation

At first glance, the meaning of open source software (hereafter referred to as OSS) may seem obvious, especially for those who are already familiar with the phrase. However, when one—even a seasoned veteran of OSS—surveys the open source landscape today, they will notice a vast and complex ecosystem. The projects, companies, and software that make up this ecosystem are each unique. Today, one will observe OSS development by hundreds of software engineers within multi-billion-dollar corporations like Google, Facebook, and Microsoft or by a single developer as a side project outside of full-time work. It seems almost impossible to imagine a technology company that doesn't rely upon, contribute to, or avail themselves of OSS in some way. The concept of OSS has developed and shifted over decades, and many who define OSS based upon previous experience find themselves having to reconceptualize what exactly OSS means. For instance, some people view OSS as the primary interest of hobbyists or tinkerers. Consequently, many also view OSS as too complicated for the general user. Still others view OSS as inferior because it doesn't seem possible that volunteers could produce an equivalent or superior software product when compared to a proprietary option. With these ideas in mind, we wish to clear away these misconceptions that obstruct one's ability to see the current landscape of OSS. To accomplish this task, we will offer a definition of OSS, consider licenses that distinguish different OSS projects, and narrate a brief and incomplete history of OSS from its origins to the current day. With an exploration of this content in hand, the reader should have the context for understanding the current state of OSS as it relates to libraries (discussed in chapter 2).

DEFINING OSS

It is important not to confuse free software and open source software. While both are similar—and the two are often conflated and referred to interchangeably as OSS—the distinctions are significant. As we will see in a later section in this chapter, licenses to use some OSS have been quite expensive and would be infeasible for an individual to license.

Likewise, matters are complicated by the confusion introduced by the ambiguous nature of the English word "free." When we speak of "free," do we mean "free" as in freedom or "free" as in without cost? Traditionally, free software, especially as articulated by advocates associated with the Free Software Foundation (FSF), qualifies as free when the user has the ability "to run, copy, distribute, study, change and improve the software."[1]

Free software, by this definition, presumes the user will have access to the software's source code in order to examine, change, improve, or redistribute the software.

Furthermore, free—also referred to as "libre"—software is not to be confused with free, as "in gratis" or "without cost." To distinguish these two ideas, some individuals refer to free, as in "without cost," software as freeware. There is no cost incurred by the user of this software, but the user also may not have access to the source code. For advocates of libre software, any software, including gratis software, is unethical if it does not come packaged with the source code and if its license doesn't permit the user to examine, experiment with, and redistribute the software.

Libre software doesn't prevent individuals or companies from using this software for commercial purposes either. In prior decades, before the increased bandwidth common in today's Internet environment, it would not have been uncommon to pay for copies of free software on media such as USB drive, CD, DVD, and even floppy disk.[2]

When we speak of free software throughout this guide, we mean free or libre software. If we mention free or gratis software, we will refer to it as freeware.

Open source software is very similar to the above definition of free software. The Open Source Initiative (OSI), an organization similar to the Free Software Foundation, considers free software and open source software to be synonymous. The choice of open source software over the term free software was a practical decision, according to the Open Source Initiative, meant to avoid the confusion inherent in the word free.[3] The Free Software Foundation, on the other hand, insists on the distinction between free software and open source software.[4]

Throughout this guide, we will use the phrase open source software, along with the acronym OSS, to refer to software whose licenses permit individuals or groups to copy, inspect, use, and improve upon it. Primarily, this distinction draws a clear line between OSS and proprietary software. Developers of proprietary software do not share the source code for the software, and proprietary licenses prohibit attempts to reverse engineer the software.

Which Open Source?

Because OSS is a complex ecosystem, the use of a single term like OSS can be misleading. The term groups together projects and communities that are quite distinct upon closer inspection. One would have to look no further than the multiplicity of OSS licenses. While software licensing may seem to consist largely of boilerplate language, OSS licenses often prove important because they demonstrate the nuances of working with, using, or distributing open source software. For example, if a developer wishes to modify and improve a piece of OSS, are they also *required* to share the modified source code changes under the same licensing terms? Can they create their own software product from the source code and profit from those changes? What a person, community, or company is permitted to do with OSS is largely spelled out in license agreements. While there are many nuances when it comes to open source licensing, the authors will primarily focus on licensing as it relates to the user of open source software, whether the user is an individual or an organization.

OPEN SOURCE LICENSING

The Open Source Initiative is the de facto authority for determining which licenses agree with open source principles. In fact, the OSI has an approval process for anyone who wishes their license to receive the stamp of approval and officially qualify as an open source license.

OSS licenses approved by the OSI fall into two broad groups: permissive and copyleft licenses.[5] As its name implies, permissive licenses are generally considered less restrictive when compared to copyleft licenses. Steven Weber, in the book *The Success of Open Source*, refers to permissive licenses as "BSD-style" licenses,[6] named after the Berkeley Software Distribution (BSD) project that pioneered this particular license. Permissive licenses have relatively few restrictions associated with them. Permissive licenses preclude warranty or liability when it comes to how the software is used. This group of licenses also requires that the originator's copyright notice be distributed with any further redistributions of the software. Apart from these restrictions, one is permitted to do whatever they wish with the software.[7] For example, one could take the source code from a BSD-licensed project, modify and build upon the code, and build a business selling the resulting code as proprietary (or close-sourced) code.

Copyleft licenses, on the other hand, are more restrictive. The prime examples of copyleft licenses are what Weber refers to as "GPL-style licenses."[8] GPL, which stands for GNU General Public License, licenses originated as an attempt in the 1970s and 1980s to counteract the growing trend in software development toward proprietary software. As a result, copyleft licenses like the GPL license restrict what licensees may do with copyleft software in order to keep the source code open and accessible to all. Primarily, copyleft licenses prevent a person from modifying, changing, and distributing copyleft software under different licensing terms than the original license. Furthermore, developers of copyleft software must make the source code accessible to all. In other words, unlike the permissive license, copyleft software cannot be made into proprietary software, no matter how many modifications are made to the software. These additional restrictions were put in place to protect the freedom of the software user interested in examining, modifying, or sharing software. Richard Stallman, the man who established the GNU project and the Free Software Foundation, also developed the GPL license. As a result, free software advocates only recognize copyleft licenses as truly free software.

For the general software user, these licensing distinctions may seem irrelevant, even though there are numerous open source licenses out there (see Table 1.1). Does it make any practical difference whether an open source product uses a permissive or copyleft license? It, in fact, does. For instance, there is nothing to prevent an individual, group, or company from using permissively licensed source code to develop a proprietary software solution or to develop business models that exclude nonpaying customers from fully accessing any enhancements to the project's documentation. Copyleft licenses, on the other hand, require derivations of copyleft-licensed software to retain similar license terms in order to prevent the sort of situations allowed by permissive licenses. Copyleft licenses prohibit a person or company from directly benefiting from open source code and not sharing any improvements or enhancements made to an OSS project. Copyleft licenses require openness and transparency. As a result, it is important for anyone who is considering implementing an open source solution to examine the license associated with that particular product. All OSS is not equal. In the following section, the history of OSS demonstrates the complexity and conflict inherent in the OSS community.

Table 1.1. Popular Open Source Applications and License Information

Popular Open Source Software	License	License Type
Android OS (Linux Kernel is GPL) Apache Hadoop Apache HTTP Server Apache Tomcat Docker	Apache License	Permissive
PHP versions 4 and higher (PHP License) Postgres/PostgreSQL (PostgreSQL License) Python (PSF Licenses) OpenRefine	BSD and BSD-style (excluding Apache or MIT)	Permissive
Drupal Git Linux OS Kernel MariaDB MySQL* Perl R WordPress	GPL – General Public License	Copyleft
jQuery Microsoft's .NET Core Node.js Ruby on Rails	MIT License	Permissive
Mozilla Firefox LibreOffice	MPL – Mozilla Public License	Partial Copyleft

A CRASH COURSE HISTORY OF OPEN SOURCE SOFTWARE

In early June 2001, Microsoft's then CEO Steve Ballmer arrived in Chicago for the launch of the company's newest office productivity software, Office XP. Among the numerous meetings with Chicago-based companies and press interviews, Ballmer met for a one-on-one interview with a reporter from the *Chicago Sun-Times* in which he likened the open source operating system Linux to a "cancer."[9] In this same interview, Ballmer additionally bemoaned government funding of open source, arguing that open source precluded corporations from using its code.[10] While Ballmer's words were, at best, inaccurate, he was right about one thing; in the nearly two decades since Ballmer uttered those words in criticism against OSS, this software ecosystem has grown exponentially in its influence, resembling more of a viral phenomenon than the cancer—with its negative connotations—Ballmer envisioned.

Not only can companies make money from OSS, but even companies who have a strong tradition of developing proprietary software like IBM and Microsoft understood the value of supporting OSS. For example, in June 2018, Microsoft announced the purchase of GitHub—one of the world's most popular platforms for sharing and contributing to OSS projects—for 7.5 billion dollars.[11] Just under five months later, Red Hat, a company built to support OSS and its enterprise users, announced that it had been acquired by IBM. The price tag: 34 billion dollars.[12] These examples, while they are outliers, demonstrate that software companies and software users can no longer afford to dismiss OSS.

In the intervening years since the turn of the twenty-first century, OSS has come to dominate the IT industry landscape, and its prevalence has only grown with the advancement of cloud computing and automation. Microsoft, as probably one of the most widely recognized software companies in the world, in just four short years (from 2015–2019) expanded from 2,000 software engineers to just under 25,000 who contribute to or use open source projects on GitHub![13] Amazon and Google both actively develop, support, and utilize OSS to run their own infrastructure and provide that same platform to numerous other companies. Whether a company specializes in web services, IT support, information security, machine learning, or even library software, OSS frequently plays an integral role in that company's continued success.

For many who do not work in the IT industry or follow it closely, these shifts have largely been overlooked, or their significance has been underestimated. For end users of traditionally developed software within the library software ecosystem, in particular, these changes can seem distant and inconsequential. In the remainder of this chapter, however, the authors hope to provide a different perspective by offering a brief history of the open source movement from its origins in the mid-twentieth century to the present day. Not only is OSS significant and omnipresent in the library ecosystem, but also libraries of all sizes and types cannot afford to dismiss the value and benefits of using and contributing to open source communities. OSS communities have as much to offer libraries as libraries have to offer OSS communities (as we will see in chapter 2). The current chapter is intended to provide the context in which to understand the current library automation landscape and the opportunities OSS projects provide the library community.

How did we get from a software environment with two seemingly polar-opposite methodologies for developing software to a software ecosystem where many companies make use of both proprietary and open source software? In hindsight, the history of almost any topic under consideration can seem predestined. Upon closer inspection, however, many contingencies are at play that drastically change the outcome of any given event. As we shall see, the OSS movement is no exception.

In the Beginning...

It is difficult to imagine a time when computers consumed the space of a large room. It may prove more surprising that these gargantuan machines came with few software tools to make efficient use of the hardware.[14] In the early days of computing, one needed to be a programmer just to use a computer. Frequently, software that did ship with these large mainframes came in the form of source code, since computer users might need to make modifications to the code in order for the programs to work as the programmers desired. For manufacturers of the hardware, it just made sense to provide the source code. Consequently, users could feel free to discard the software that shipped with these machines and create their own if they were willing to commit the time. In 1969, two researchers at Bell Technology Laboratories, a research arm of AT&T in the late twentieth century, would do just that.

When the collaborative efforts of several labs, including Bell Labs, to develop the operating system called Multics failed, Ken Thompson and Dennis Ritchie worked to develop an alternative operating system within Bell Labs. This operating system came to be known as Unix. The popularity of Unix grew in the years following its inception for a variety of reasons. First, Unix's early success was due in no small part to AT&T's consent decree with the US federal government limiting the company and its subsidiaries from pursuing profit outside of telephone services. In the second place—and as a result of the previous factor—AT&T licensed Unix for a comparatively small fee to academic institutions and researchers. Third, Unix was shipped to licensees as source code, and AT&T provided no support for the operating system. As Steven Weber has noted, these factors served to foster an environment of information sharing and assistance among licensees.[15] Finally, by the mid-1970s, Unix was mostly developed in the high-level programming language C, a language also developed by Bell Labs researchers who worked on the Unix project. This development made Unix portable to other hardware than the machine on which it had initially been developed.[16] All of these factors, in addition to the continually decreasing cost of mainframes, made Unix appealing to a broad group of users. Unix administrators and programmers could share their knowledge and improvements with each other. This situation, however, wouldn't last long. As legal circumstances changed for AT&T in the 1980s, the Unix ecosystem that had developed over a decade would be threatened. Fortunately, Bell Labs wasn't the only key stakeholder on the block. As the next two sections show, from Berkeley, California, to Cambridge, Massachusetts, hackers and computer science students were willing to put in the work to keep Unix code freely available well into the future.[17]

Richard Stallman, the GNU Project, and the Fight to Free Software

Richard Stallman had had enough. For over a decade, this young man had spent much of his time learning at the feet of MIT's notorious group of hackers, a group of young men who valued the free sharing of information and cleverness in computer programming. For them, working with mainframes and bending them to your will was its own reward. As a freshman student at Harvard University in 1970, Stallman would visit the Artificial Intelligence (AI) Lab at the Massachusetts Institute of Technology (MIT). At MIT, Stallman found acceptance among a group of veteran hackers and imbibed the culture of openness and learning.[18] By 1983, the community of hackers where Stallman had a sense of belonging—and of which he considered himself to be the final true member—would be torn apart by what he considered to be greedy corporate interests and the quest to capitalize on advancements in computing.[19] In response, Stallman announced, in 1983, a new project to fight back against the growing trend of nondisclosure agreements and closed-source software distributions.[20] His goal? To create a completely free (as in freedom) operating system based on the Unix operating system so popular among academic and research institutions. Stallman would call this project GNU (short for GNU's Not Unix). Beginning in 1984, Stallman would quit his job at MIT's AI lab and pursue developing the GNU project full-time. As a further response, and in conjunction with the GNU project, Stallman developed a license to protect the rights of software users and to keep software free. In the years that followed, Stallman and programmer advocates who rallied around the free software cause would make great strides in bringing the project to fruition. However, the GNU project was missing one critical piece: the operating system's kernel. Without a kernel, Stallman's quest to develop a *complete*, free operating system would fail. As the years passed and the GNU project developers failed to deliver a workable kernel, the GNU hope seemed lost. Fortunately for Stallman and GNU project participants, a young Finnish student from Helsinki was across the Atlantic hacking away to solve this very problem. But before we consider the phenomenon that was to become known as the Linux kernel, let us consider another project that grew out of the period of accessibility and learning made possible by Unix.

Notorious BSD

When Ken Thompson and Dennis Ritchie, two of the primary developers of Unix, first presented details of their operating system in 1973 to attendees of the Fourth Association for Computing Machinery (ACM) Symposium on Operating Systems, they received a warm response. By 1977, over 500 sites were using Unix. Many of these sites were educational institutions like the University of

California at Berkeley.[21] UC Berkeley, Thompson's alma mater, would become a key contributor to the development of Unix in the following decades.

UC Berkeley would become such a crucial partner in the development of Unix that the Computer Systems Research Group (CSRG) at Berkeley began distributing Unix enhancements under their own license. Any institution that had a license to the underlying Unix code upon which the Berkeley software had been developed could also make use of the Berkeley software.

When, in 1979, Bell Labs modified the licensing terms of its newest release of Unix, version 7, CSRG responded by forking the Unix source code prior to the version 7 release and releasing the third major version of its software distribution as a complete operating system. This distribution was known at the time as 3BSD.

BSD, at this point in its development, was limited in terms of distribution. BSD could only be distributed to other sites with a Unix license, and by 1988, the Unix license price tag had skyrocketed up to $100,000.[22] As a result, the improvements the CSRG had made to Unix were difficult to distribute to all interested parties. In 1989, after a successful release of the TCP/IP code alone, referred to as Networking Release 1, the CSRG developed a plan to reverse-engineer all of the underlying AT&T code that ran BSD and distribute it under a permissive license.[23] In less than two years, and with the contributions of almost 400 developers scattered geographically, CSRG had almost completely written AT&T code out of the next BSD release.[24] When it was released in 1991, CSRG's latest release of the BSD code would be called Networking Release 2, even though it was almost a complete system free of Unix code in its own right. An individual named Bill Jolitz took the Networking Release 2 code, wrote code to replace the six omitted files with AT&T original code in it, and started distributing copies of what came to be known as 386/BSD on the Internet. As its name implies, 386/BSD was a distribution of BSD specifically designed to work with Intel 386 processors. Thus, Jolitz not only distributed BSD under the same permissive licensing terms as previous versions of BSD, but he also brought a full-featured Unix-like system to a processing architecture that was destined to dominate PCs.[25] These developments, among others, would lead the CSRG in particular and the University of California system in general into a legal battle in 1992.[26] While BSD would survive into the present, concerns over the fate of BSD slowed its advancement in the early 1990s. Luckily, BSD wasn't the only project under development.

The Rise of Linux

Jolitz's project wasn't the only one to bring a Unix-like operating system to a PC-compatible architecture, however. In response to the licensing changes

AT&T made with the release of Unix version 7, computer science professor Andrew Tanenbaum would develop his own Unix-like operating system called Minix from scratch.[27] Tanenbaum created Minix as an educational tool for students to better comprehend how operating systems work since the new Unix license didn't allow students access to the source code. When Tanenbaum had completed Minix in 1986, he began to distribute the source code at a comparatively minimal cost. In 1991, a computer science student at the University of Helsinki named Linus Torvalds discovered Minix when a course textbook published by Tanenbaum made extensive use of Minix code to explain operating systems.[28]

Because Minix was created primarily as a teaching tool, Tanenbaum was reluctant to make significant changes to Minix.[29] It was winter in Helsinki, and Torvalds, wishing to access his university's Unix mainframe remotely, decided to develop his own terminal emulator program that communicated directly with his computer's hardware and not on top of Minix. Torvald's reasons for this were twofold. On the one hand, he was not satisfied with Minix when it came to terminal emulation. On the other hand, developing his terminal emulation program on top of the hardware of his new computer would give him an opportunity to acquaint himself with the computer architecture.[30] It was this curiosity that ultimately launched what would become Linux. In less than a year, Torvalds would launch version 0.01 of what would become known as the Linux kernel. By 1994, Torvalds and numerous developers from all over the world had added enough functionality for Torvalds to release version 1.0. Over the years and in the following decades, Linux has remained true to the principle of a free (as in cost) kernel. The development model that organically arose from the Linux kernel is still largely intact today and is utilized by numerous other open source projects.

While Torvalds and the other hackers worked to improve and develop the Linux kernel, other Linux supporters began to package many of the GNU utilities with the Linux kernel. Similar projects across the world would spawn what came to be known as Linux distributions, with each distribution representing a particular vision of what a fully functioning operating system should be. Some of the most enduring distributions that persist today from this early period include Debian GNU/Linux, Red Hat Enterprise Linux, and OpenSUSE.

Apache, MySQL, and the Ps

Linux could not have succeeded alone, and OSS wouldn't have become a movement if other software projects hadn't seen the value of the open source development model. Numerous other OSS that sprang up in the 1990s helped to solidify the OSS movement as a dominant player in the domain of IT infrastructure and software development. Tools like the Apache web server, the MySQL relational database, and programming languages like Perl, Python, and PHP all helped to establish the GNU/Linux operating system as critical infrastructure at the beginning of the millennium.[31]

The Apache HTTP server, for example, grew out of the collaborative efforts of webmasters to maintain the successful National Center for Supercomputing Applications (NCSA) web server after its maintainers left the NCSA for work elsewhere. What grew out of these efforts would come to be known as the Apache HTTP server and the Apache Group, a body of key stakeholders responsible for the maintenance and direction of the Apache HTTP server. The Apache HTTP server has its own open source development model distinct from the model popularized by Linux.[32]

MySQL, one of the most popular open source relational databases on the market, has its own unique development and licensing model as well. First released in 1996 by Monty Widenius and David Axmark, MySQL was distributed with both a proprietary and an open source license. Additionally, almost all development of MySQL was handled in-house by paid developers for MySQL's controlling company, MySQL AB.[33] This behavior is in stark contrast to many of the previous models for open source development discussed earlier in this chapter. To further add complications, MySQL was purchased by Sun Microsystems in 2008 for $1 billion.[34] Just over a year later, Oracle would purchase Sun Microsystems.[35] With the uncertainty these frequent changes introduced, Widenius forked the MySQL code and developed MariaDB to ensure that his project would remain open source.[36]

Perl, PHP, and Python are all examples of powerful open source programming languages. With the advent of these languages in the late 1980s and early in the 1990s, developers could use any of these languages in conjunction with MySQL, Apache, and Linux to develop a free, full-featured web application. Even today, the Linux, Apache, MySQL, Perl/Python/PHP (LAMP) stack is still a tried-and-true method for developing web applications.

The success of these tools in forming a large portion of the Internet backbone demonstrated not only that open source methods of software development were sustainable but also that they often sped up the rate at which improvements to IT infrastructure occurred.

Computers Great and Small (Linux Spreads to Mobile and Into the Cloud)

It is difficult to underestimate the impact Linux, the GNU project, and the other open source server applications from the 1990s had on the history of information technology. Just as important as the software that resulted from these open source projects were the development models that originated from them.

Linux, as the prime example, demonstrated that releasing software frequently and early, even when it still contained bugs, often improved the overall quality of software products.[37] Instead of diminishing its value, this approach to development transformed users into contributors to the project. With the advent of the Internet, the Linux kernel was able to benefit from global expertise as well. The days of requiring in-person collaboration on software development were gone.[38] Finally, even though the Linux license was a copyleft license, numerous companies grew up around Linux. As the history of Linux makes clear, OSS wasn't inherently antithetical to business. Companies like Red Hat and MySQL are perfect examples of the financial success companies can have while also sharing source code with its users.

Since the year 2000, companies have found new ways to incorporate OSS development into their operations. With the rise of cloud computing in the previous decade, companies began to sell subscription services to their OSS, referred to as Software as a Service (SaaS).[39] Thus, cloud computing allowed companies to reap the benefits of a dedicated community who were willing to download and manage the software for free on their own and a much larger community that values the convenience of having software managed for them.

The OSS movement is a complex and diverse environment. Licensing terms often make a significant difference in what end users and companies are able to do with OSS, and development models for open source projects vary as well. After over half of a century when academics and researchers used to share code freely for educational purposes, the method of transparency remains integral to the advancement of information technology still today. In comparison, traditional proprietary models of software development are rarely sufficient at delivering quick, innovative technologies to market. The library automation market is no exception to this observation. As the next chapter shows, OSS provides alternatives in the library automation ecosystem that are healthy for both companies and libraries.

NOTES

1. "What is Free Software?" GNU Operating System, Free Software Foundation, accessed February 11, 2020, https://www.gnu.org/philosophy/free-sw.en.html.

2. You can still purchase current versions of GNU/Linux software online in many of these formats.

3. "What is 'Free Software' and is it the Same as 'Open Source?'" Frequently Answered Questions, Open Source Initiative, accessed February 11, 2020, https://opensource.org/faq#free-software.

4. "What is Free Software?" Free Software Foundation.

5. Heather Meeker, "Open Source Licensing: What Every Technologist Should Know," *Opensource.com*, September 21, 2017, https://opensource.com/article/17/9/open-source-licensing.

6. Steven Weber, *The Success of Open Source* (Cambridge, MA: Harvard University Press, 2004), 181.

7. Meeker, "Open Source Licensing."

8. Weber, *The Success of Open Source*, 181.

9. It has been noted by Cristopher Tozzi that Ballmer's exaggeration of free and open source software was intentional and meant to sway public opinion against free and open source software. Certainly, Ballmer's statements about free and open source software at least misconstrue free and open source licensing and the complexities inherent in that domain. For a more detailed discussion of Microsoft and its relationship with free and open source software, see Christopher Tozzi, *For Fun and Profit: A History of the Free and Open Source Software Revolution* (Cambridge, MA: MIT Press, 2017), 211–40.

10. Dave Newbart, "Microsoft CEO Takes Launch Break with the Sun-Times," *Chicago Sun-Times,* June 1, 2001, accessed January 31, 2020, https://web.archive.org/web/20010606035140/ and http://www.suntimes.com/output/tech/cst-fin-micro01.html.

11. "Microsoft to Acquire GitHub for $7.5 Billion," *Microsoft News Center*, Microsoft, Inc., June 4, 2018, https://news.microsoft.com/2018/06/04/microsoft-to-acquire-github-for-7-5-billion/.

12. "IBM to Acquire Red Hat, Completely Changing the Cloud Landscape and Becoming World's #1 Hybrid Cloud Provider," Red Hat, Inc., October 28, 2018, https://www.redhat.com/en/about/press-releases/ibm-acquire-red-hat-completely-changing-cloud-landscape-and-becoming-worlds-1-hybrid-cloud-provider.

13. Jeff Wilcox, "Scaling from 2,000 to 25,000 engineers on GitHub at Microsoft," *Jeff Wilcox* (blog), June 25, 2019, https://www.jeff.wilcox.name/2019/06/scaling-25k/.

14. Weber, *The Success of Open Source*, 21.

15. Weber, 28–9.

16. Fadi P. Deek and James A. M. McHugh, *Open Source: Technology and Policy* (Cambridge, MA: University of Cambridge Press, 2008), 81.

17. While the term hacker nowadays carries a negative connotation with it, the origin of the term can be traced back to post-World War II MIT. Hackers, throughout most of the history of that term, referred to a person who devised ingenious methods for solving difficult problems. For more information on the term hacker, see Stallman's online article at https://stallman.org/articles/on-hacking.html.

18. Steven Levy, *Hackers: Heroes of the Computer Revolution* (New York: Penguin Books, 1984), 415.

19. Levy, *Hackers*, 421–27.

20. "Initial Announcement," GNU Operating System, Free Software Foundation, accessed February 14, 2020, https://www.gnu.org/gnu/initial-announcement.en.html.

21. Deek and McHugh, *Open Source*, 83.

22. Weber, *The Success of Open Source*, 39–40.

23. TCP/IP is a set of protocols forming the backbone of the modern-day Internet. While it is not the only protocol suite for computer networking, it has become the industry standard.

24. Only six files with AT&T code remained in Networking Release 2.

25. Weber, *The Success of Open Source*, 42.

26. Weber, *The Success of Open Source*, 43.

27. Glyn Moody, *Rebel Code: Inside Linux and the Open Source Revolution* (Cambridge, MA: Perseus Publishing, 2001), 33–34.

28. Moody, *Rebel Code*, 31–32.

29. Linus Torvalds and David Diamond, *Just for Fun: The Story of an Accidental Revolutionary* (New York: HarperBusiness, 2001), 61–62.

30. Torvalds and Diamond, *Just for Fun*, 62.

31. GNU/Linux is a way of referring to the Linux kernel in addition to the GNU utilities. Taken together, these components constitute a full-fledged operating system.

32. Deek and McHugh, *Open Source*, 24–30.

33. Deek and McHugh, *Open Source*, 64–65.

34. Jeremy Kirk, "Sun to Acquire MySQL for $1 Billion," *PC World*, January 16, 2008, https://www.pcworld.com/article/141409/article.html.

35. "Oracle Buys Sun," Oracle, Inc., April 20, 2009, https://www.oracle.com/corporate/pressrelease/oracle-buys-sun-042009.html.

36. "About MariaDB Server," MariaDB Foundation, accessed on February 17, 2020, https://mariadb.org/about/.

37. Eric S. Raymond, *The Cathedral and the Bazaar: Musings on Linux and Open Source by an Accidental Revolutionary* (Sebastopol, CA: O'Reilly, 1999), 38–39.

38. Tozzi, *For Fun and Profit*, 159–61.

39. Mike Volpi, "How Open Source Software Took Over the World," *TechCrunch*, January 12, 2019, https://techcrunch.com/2019/01/12/how-open-source-software-took-over-the-world/.

2

Open Source Software in Libraries

The Texas A&M campus in College Station, Texas, does not let you forget at any point that you are, in fact, in the very heart of Texas. "Howdy" is the only acceptable greeting, Kyle Field and the home of the 12th Man, many of the 60,000-plus students (or Aggies, as they are referred) are dressed for business, and the grass is so perfect that perhaps only Hank Hill could truly appreciate its beauty. It's also the site of the forward-thinking Texas A&M Libraries and, as a result, an international gathering of librarians, developers, and library service providers working to fundamentally change how libraries have operated since the mid-twentieth century.

In 2020, the Open Library Foundation (hereafter referred to as OLF) celebrated its fifth year in existence. While the concept of open source software (OSS) isn't a new phenomenon within the library ecosystem, this foundation's existence—along with the conference it maintains, the World Open Library Foundation Conference (WOLFcon)—marks a significant milestone of the OSS movement within libraries. Created in 2016, the OLF and its conference are the first attempts within the library world to bring together several OSS library software communities and to increase the accessibility of OSS and open access projects.[1] While the OLF is a relative newcomer to the library OSS ecosystem, its existence as an organization dedicated to facilitating OSS development in the library community is a welcome sight to OSS advocates.[2]

The establishment of the OLF is not an anomaly but is instead a result of significant technological shifts relevant to libraries. While the earliest library-centric OSS applications have been in existence since the turn of the twenty-first century, technological advancements in network bandwidth, cloud computing, and computer programming—to name just a few—have only expanded the potential software solutions available to libraries. These new technologies and the business models that have popped up around them also allow OSS developers, communities, and advocates to address the historic difficulties in the adoption of OSS applications. While these changes are relatively recent in libraries, they are quickly picking up speed, with many general industry business models to serve as examples from which to learn and emulate. Indeed, the evolving pattern in libraries mirrors the overall OSS movement and adoption patterns at large discussed in the first chapter.

This technological advancement, along with support within the library community for OSS, didn't occur in a vacuum. Rather, the current state of OSS library systems is the result of decades of work in the area of automation, communications, and infrastructure. While many librarians may be familiar with some aspects of these advancements, few connections seem to have been drawn between the history of library automation technology at the end of the twentieth century and the current state of library software. The rest of this chapter seeks to provide a brief history of library automation and connect the history of library software with the development of OSS library software in its current state. Following that, we will explore the real-world benefits and challenges of implementing OSS in libraries. Finally, we will make a case for OSS as a legitimate model for developing real-world software that meets the needs, and is responsive to, libraries in the twenty-first century.

HISTORY

To better understand the current state of OSS in libraries, we must first understand the history of library systems and library automation in general. For a high-level historical view, Thomas Kochtanek and Joseph Matthews, in 2002, described four overlapping areas of development for library systems in the first edition of *Library Information Systems* that the authors of this guide find useful: the Systems era, the Functionality era, the End User era, and the Globalization of Information Resources era.[3] In the second edition of *Library Information Systems*, published in 2020, Joseph Matthews and Carson Block appended two additional eras to the four: the Discovery Systems era and the Knowledge Innovation era.[4]

The Systems Era was composed of the earliest automation efforts with heavy reliance on proprietary hardware and software to mimic paper-based or manual workflows in the library, such as circulation control.[5] This era lasted from the 1950s into the 1970s. The era of Functionality (1960s–1980s) commercialized many of the advancements individuals and organizations developed and helped to transform library automation tasks to include many other areas of library operations like serials control, acquisitions, cataloging, and the computer-based, or online, catalog culminating in applications we know today as the Integrated Library System, or the ILS.[6] The pioneering individuals and organizations that were active in these eras laid the foundations that libraries, for the most part, still operate within today, including our partnership-like relationships with vendors who develop library systems software. There is also evidence that library automation transformed the division of labor within libraries and helped define what a contemporary library is.[7] While neither are topics covered in this guide, it does demonstrate the impact information technology development has on libraries isn't limited to the disruption to libraries caused by the appearance and wild success that is the World Wide Web.

Whereas the Systems and Functionality eras supported and transformed the internal operations of the library, the middle two eras—End User (1980s–1990s) and Globalization of Information Resources (1990s–2000s)—focused on making the online catalog, commonly known as online public access catalog (OPAC), accessible directly to the library patron with little to no assistance from library personnel. The Globalization era pushed this further with the assistance of the World Wide Web and more advanced Internet networking technologies and standards. The technology of the World Wide Web and increased interconnectivity served to integrate library catalogs, online databases, and digital content. The result of these dramatic technological shifts was that library resources, still mostly print-based but increasingly digital, were made more discoverable and accessible than they had ever been before. From banking and finance, healthcare, education, as well as shopping and entertainment, many other industries have followed the same path that the End User and Globalization era of library systems development describes. Putting the end-user in control with access to services 24/7 from anywhere on virtually any device is now the expectation of most users and consumers.

The Discovery Systems era marked the waning importance of physical library collections and, as a result, the weakening of the ILS as the library's main system for managing costs, inventory control, and user transactions. The appearance of web-scale discovery services that utilize index and knowledgebase technologies to provide a single place to discover all of the content available has helped push the balance in libraries away from print to electronic assets. Due to the changing nature from print-based to digital- or electronic-based resources as well as methods of access and discovery made available by high rates of adoption of the Internet and even the fast rate of change in hardware available for users to accomplish these tasks, many other systems appeared around the 2000s to the 2010s to better manage these new types of resources and their accessibility while the development of new ILS functionality was slow to respond. At the same time that library collections were shifting to primarily electronic resources, a change in ownership models was also occurring. Instead of libraries owning copies of content, resource providers were moving to offer licensed, limited access to electronic-based content. During this phase, the Electronic Resource Management System (ERMS) came into existence to assist in handling the complex licensing terms and to manage content that no longer physically existed in the library's collection. The ERMS is just one instance of software developed in response to the new realities presented by the Internet revolution. Other systems of note that appeared during this era include OpenURL link resolvers, Digital Asset Management Systems (DAMS), Institutional Repositories (IR), and Discovery Service Layers.

The most forward-thinking ILS vendors largely responded to these changes in two ways: by acquiring and merging with one another or by developing the Library Services Platform (LSP). In some cases, vertical integration efforts have been made between ILS providers and database providers. Specific examples of these two strategies include Proquest's acquisition of Ex Libris, the creator of the Alma LSP, in 2015; OCLC's development of the LSP—Worldshare Management Services (WMS)—in 2010; and EBSCO's financial support and sponsorship of efforts to integrate OSS projects (e.g., the Koha ILS and the FOLIO LSP currently under development) with EBSCO's database and discovery products. Dubbed by Marshall Breeding as the Library Services Platform, LSPs are generally defined as multi-tenant, web-scale systems.[8] They represent ILS vendor's attempts to once again unify the disparate modules/systems a library needs to adequately manage its collections and interactions with its patrons. LSPs, for the most part, offer better options for integration and focus on e-resource management while still supporting traditional print management needs. However, they are still far outnumbered by ILSs and often come at a higher cost than a traditional ILS. Because of their unified, all-in-one nature, they also perpetuate some of the issues ILSs introduced, including painful and costly migrations, of which many libraries continue to be apprehensive. The Discovery Systems era was active with many new innovations in library systems. Many of these innovations were made possible by the general OSS movement, and the growth of library OSS systems during this time reflects that.

CURRENT STATE

While OSS ILSs appeared mostly from the commoditization, increasing costs, and vendor lock-in frustrations of the ILS market, OSS, home-grown

IRs, DAMS, discovery layers, and archival management software, just to name a few, appeared either concurrently or before proprietary systems.[9] There are a number of reasons for this difference. Unlike the ILS, these new systems weren't designed to replicate manual functions already happening in a library; they didn't require cost-prohibitive hardware that the earliest library information systems did; the Internet increased the speed and reach for communicating and exchanging information than ever before; and, finally, the underlying foundational software like web services, database management systems, and OS for applications to run on were not only available but also widely accessible as OSS or freeware/shareware licensed applications. These developments enabled a variety of interested individuals or parties to address their own software needs at a much lower cost without requiring partnerships with vendors. Importantly, this applied not only to the OSS applications that came into existence but also the proprietary systems that appeared at this time were often built on the same open core software and the LAMP stack (or LAMP-like) architecture.[10]

For the OSS apprehensive, the authors believe it is worth noting that today virtually all proprietary library systems use OSS core technologies described in chapter 1 of this guide. The only exceptions are typically at the database management system level, with some vendors still using Oracle and others, in niche areas of library systems, using Microsoft's suite of applications. Aside from many vendors relying on various distributions of the OSS operating system (OS), Linux, most vendors also rely on OSS high-level programming languages, web services, and database management systems like the aforementioned LAMP stack.[11] In fact, many proprietary ILSs in use, according to data gathered from Marshall Breeding's *Library Technology Guides*, rely on one or more OSS applications. By using these OSS applications, the vendors benefit in a number of ways. The most notable benefit to vendors is the significant cost savings from either not having to license a particular product or not having to spend the development time and money that would be required to develop their own core applications. Additionally, many of these applications hold the majority of market share in their particular domains. As a result, the vendors also benefit from the standardization that comes with using these applications as well as a larger pool of talent familiar with using these systems on the development and management side of their operations. Lastly, these OSS applications have large communities supporting and contributing to them. Critical aspects of any application like stability and security are addressed by individuals and teams working in those particular areas of expertise and then passed on to all for patches and new releases. (As chapter 1 illustrates, this behavior stems not only from kindness or a sense of community but is required by many OSS licenses.)

What is clear is that proprietary library software vendors are well aware of the benefits of using OSS.

WHY CHOOSE OSS?

Even though the OSS development model has historically, as outlined in the previous section, been proven to be a legitimate and competitive methodology both within the software landscape in general and in the library software landscape in particular, many library stakeholders are still skeptical of OSS library software. In a modest attempt to address what we perceive to be the most common objections, the section that follows poses these objections as subheadings. In the text that follows, the authors then attempt to provide a cogent and fair response to what are reasonable concerns when it comes to considering OSS library software options.

The risks involved in using OSS are too great.

One of the main arguments against OSS adoption is the perceived risk involved with using software where there is no single company responsible for its development. It's true that free and OSS applications have no immediate costs, but they are not cost-free. They are often described as "free like a puppy not free like lunch" or, as Richard Stallman has described, "think free as in free speech, not free beer."[12] However, just like any proprietary application, an OSS application cannot or should not be judged by the application itself. An individual or organization must evaluate the ecosystem around an application. Indeed, this guide is not intended to be a call to use OSS solutions indiscriminately or for the sake of them being OSS. There are many occasions where a proprietary application would not only serve the users better but also be a sound decision from a cost and risk control point of view. Whereas for a proprietary application an evaluator must consider the overall health of the commercial organization and the quality of support and development, an evaluator looking at an OSS application must evaluate the community that is using and developing the application as well as businesses or service providers that support the OSS application in other ways. Other aspects of many successful OSS projects to carefully consider are a project's governance structure, its participating members, and the type of OSS license being used.

We don't have the in-house technical expertise to manage OSS.

This objection is similar to what's required to evaluate risk. Just like a proprietary application, an OSS application cannot be judged by the application itself. It should also be judged by the community surrounding it, including the organizations that provide dedicated support or development for an application. Regarding community, do libraries of a similar size and type effectively use and positively evaluate the software? How many service providers exist for the software, and what type of services do they provide? What tools are available to communicate with the community and set short-term and long-term goals for a project's development? These questions and how they are answered will give any evaluator a good idea of what type of in-house technical expertise will actually be required for such an application. If the community is composed of multiple similarly sized libraries that are mostly happy with the application, the depth of technical expertise may be lessened by the support available from the community. If there are multiple service providers providing numerous services such as hosting, support, training, migration, implementation, and custom development with a healthy amount of customers/clients, this is another indicator that no greater in-house technical expertise would be expected for an OSS solution than with a proprietary system. Many library OSS options fall within a spectrum for these variables. Becoming familiar with an application's community and service provider options will allow an evaluator to more accurately anticipate the technical expertise required.[13]

The software doesn't do X, or *We need a more robust system to meet our needs.*

There are many strategies for determining the requirements a library has for an application or system. No matter what application is under consideration, when conducting a gap-analysis or comparing the options, there invariably are functions or workflows that are different or missing entirely that require a change by library personnel to successfully adopt and use the new system. In the authors' experiences, this is the case for both proprietary and OSS applications. However, as an OSS project is more transparent and encourages improvement to its source code, gaps or issues are easier to identify and address than proprietary options and often earlier in the process. Vendors of proprietary systems can sometimes obscure the limitations of their software during a sales pitch, whether intentional or due to a misunderstanding of functional need. Mapping and weighing the importance of certain features ahead of time is crucial to determining whether a particular component is needed for library operations. Depending on the OSS application, the options to develop custom features in-house or fast-track development by crowdsourcing an enhancement opens avenues to libraries that haven't previously existed with proprietary library software. Except for the largest contracts or prominent, well-known libraries, this type of development is rarely an option for proprietary applications. Additionally, if the community of an OSS project is robust and composed of similar organizations, community-generated workarounds or solutions may already exist to address perceived or very real limitations.

It's worth noting that a library using a proprietary software solution benefits the other users of that software as well, but the path of development, customization, or improvement is not dictated by a community. It is dictated by a commercial organization with priorities and a strategy that may not benefit its current customers. There is no guarantee a vendor will listen to the concerns or needs of its customers. There is no guarantee a vendor will not merge or be acquired by a competitor with a different strategy. Finally, recall that many proprietary options are built on the same OSS core technologies as completely OSS options. Though the underlying components of a system can impact how well a system scales up or down to fit an organization's needs and being aware of those limitations is important, often it's not that a system's underlying components aren't able to perform x or do y; it's more likely the development path or strategy taken doesn't easily or cheaply accommodate adding the missing functionality or robustness.

We need systems and software applications that align with our values.

While this assertion isn't an explicit concern stated by library stakeholders, we believe this concern is often implied when discussions of the current library software ecosystem arise. These stakeholders often find themselves staring in the OSS universe striving for the above desired outcome. That's not surprising. The OSS movement aligns with several of the ALA's Core Values of Librarianship, especially the stated values of public good, sustainability, and social responsibility.[14] While ideally these would be the only criteria for selecting any tool or resource, librarians interested in implementing new software must also review and select solutions based on user and community needs.

What are the total costs?

Two common pain points converge when libraries consider migrating or implementing a library software solution. These factors consist of stagnant or decreased funding and rising annual costs for licensed content. Reinforcing anecdotal evidence libraries see during the renewal process, research indicates that licensed content is steadily rising annually anywhere from 5 to 10 percent.[15] While OSS solutions can offer cost savings, especially when using applications with robust and active communities around them, they do not eliminate all costs. Instead of paying a company for a support and licensing fee to use their software, an organization may instead need to contract with a support provider or hire an expert to work directly for the organization. As library software providers are generally for-profit, publicly traded, or privately held companies not based within a library's state or region, a library has the opportunity to spend less while funneling resources into communities whose interests more closely align with libraries.

GLOBAL IMPACT

Libraries adopting OSS where available and appropriate is not only a win for the organization and its users, but it also positively impacts the entire community of an application's users. While adoption of OSS library software has generally consisted of small and/or budget-stressed libraries, when a larger library decides to invest in OSS, that library's resources available for development and/or support have an immediate impact on all current and future users. Some of the largest adoption rates of OSS in general and specific to libraries have been outside of the United States. The Koha ILS previously mentioned, for example, is the number one installed ILS in the world, with nearly three-quarters (73 percent) of those installs being outside the United States (Library Technology Guides, 2020). American libraries helped develop the earliest library systems, and many commercial companies in operation are based in the United States. Perhaps it is not surprising that libraries in the United States, being so well established, would be the slowest to move to applications some still consider risky. However, from library values invoking community and social justice, there is much to be gained by working toward higher adoption rates of OSS applications in the United States. An argument can also be made that US libraries adopting OSS applications would have a beneficial impact on libraries internationally as well. Not including the large development possibilities many US libraries and service providers are in a good position to fund, collectively, as more US libraries adopted OSS, there would be more documentation, more support, and more language and translation work taken on. Over time, small, individual contributions such as these to a project's community have a very large overall positive impact. Widespread global use of OSS options with this type of participation could have lasting impacts on developing international standards and workflows that the systems evolve to support.

SUMMARY

The first chapter in this guide discussed the history of the free and OSS movement, including the reasons or motivations of the individuals and organizations that work on these projects. One of the challenges for libraries in this regard is that they have been utilizing information systems and technology for longer than many other industries, and as a result, they have been slower to respond to innovations such as the Cloud or SaaS Platforms made possible by faster bandwidth network connections, cheap storage, and remote-based collaboration upon which most modern organizations thrive.[16] But the new systems libraries have willed into existence in the last fifteen years tied to management, discovery, and access to electronic resources and born-digital items have had a significant impact on libraries' participation in the OSS realm.

The remaining chapters of this guide will discuss in detail specific library management systems, popular applications, OSS options, and descriptions of the communities and service providers that support those OSS options. The reader should gain a better understanding of what OSS really is, what options are available, their pros and cons for different types of libraries, and what to consider when reviewing a library OSS system.

NOTES

1. "About Us," Open Library Foundation, accessed January 22, 2020, https://openlibraryfoundation.org/.
2. Ibid.
3. Thomas R. Kochtanek and Joseph R. Matthews, *Library Information Systems: From Library Automation to Distributed Information Access Solutions* (Westport, CT: Libraries Unlimited, 2002), 6–7.
4. Joseph R. Matthews and Carson Block, *Library Information Systems* (Santa Barbara, CA: Libraries Unlimited, 2020), 7–8. Libraries are in the early stages of the Knowledge Innovation era. This era can be described as a library's attempt at incubating and supporting knowledge creation, whether it be through publishing works including those that are open access (OA) including open educational resources (OER), showcasing or exhibiting unique collections that bring to light local history or culture, or creation of a space commonly called a makerspace, a lab equipped to support the learning or practice of art, science, and commerce with tools for content creation as well as physical tool and product creation. While the Knowledge Innovation era is not the specific focus on this guide, the era is important to be aware of as it will likely only accelerate the introduction, adoption, creation, and experimentation of OSS solutions in libraries.

5. Circulation control is a manual or automated library workflow that manages loaning materials to library patrons and, under which, policies. This requires keeping a record on every item and every patron including contact details, when items are loaned out, when they are due back, and penalties when items are not returned by the due date.

6. Acquisitions: Within libraries and library systems, acquisitions is the process, work group, and/or module within an ILS of ordering, processing, and adding items to a library's collections. Cataloging: Within libraries cataloging or bibliographic control is the process of describing a record being added to a library's collections. This includes a large range of data describing the item or metadata for proper classification and location within collection. Fields like title, author, subject, call number, and publisher and publish date are often crucial for successful discovery and access of both print and electronic items. Serials Control: Area in ILS for inventory of serials issues, processing newly arrived items, and managing subscriptions and their issue frequency schedule.

7. Hugh C. Atkinson, "Who Will Run and Use Libraries? How?" *Library Journal* 109, no. 17 (1984): 1905–7; Sean C. Burns, "Academic Libraries and Automation: A Historical Reflection on Ralph Halsted Parker," *portal: Libraries and the Academy* 14, no. 1 (2014): 87–102.

8. Marshall Breeding, "New Library Collections, New Technologies, New Workflows," *Computers in Libraries* 32, no. 6 (2012): 23–25.

9. Commoditization: Based on Deek and McHugh's definition in *Open Source Technology and Policy*—"occurs when one product is pretty much like another or at least good enough for the needs it serves."; Vendor lock-in: Based on Deek and McHugh's definition in *Open Source Technology and Policy*—"A user of a product is said to be locked-in to a particular brand if the direct and indirect costs of switching to another brand are prohibitive."; To be discussed in detail in chapter 3 of this guide.

10. LAMP: A server application architecture that utilizes **L**inux OS, **A**pache Web Services, **M**ySQL Relational Database Management System, and **P**HP high-level object-oriented programming language (all open source) as components for a web-based application. LAMP-like applications are built similarly to LAMP stacks but will substitute one or more of AMP of the LAMP stack with other open source options.

11. Linux, from the Wikipedia article of same name, "is a family of open-source Unix-like operating systems based on the Linux kernel, an operating system kernel first released on September 17, 1991, by Linus Torvalds," accessed November 9, 2020, https://en.wikipedia.org/wiki/Linux.

12. "Gratis versus libre," Wikipedia, accessed November 9, 2020, https://en.wikipedia.org/wiki/Gratis_versus_libre.

13. The following chapters of this guide will cover in detail all facets of using OSS in libraries.

14. "Core Values of Librarianship," American Library Association, accessed January 23, 2020, http://www.ala.org/advocacy/intfreedom/corevalues.

15. Stephen Bosch, Barbara Albee, and Sion Romaine, "Deal or No Deal | Periodicals Price Survey 2019," *Library Journal,* April 04, 2019, https://www.libraryjournal.com/?detailStory=Deal-or-No-Deal-Periodicals-Price-Survey-2019.

16. The cloud is a generic term referring to the storage of data and applications on servers in data centers. SaaS, or Software as a Service, is a cloud-based application or suite of applications. From Phil Simon, *Age of the Platform: How Amazon, Apple, Facebook, and Google Have Redefined Business,* S.I. Publishing (Henderson, NV: Motion Publishing, 2011), Kindle Edition, locations 734–40.

3

Open Source ILS

The Integrated Library System (ILS) is the foundation of library automation and information systems in libraries. Correspondingly, it is the most mature type of library system and, of all library systems, best represents the culmination of the library automation development that began in earnest in the 1960s. Their impact on libraries is such that over time library operations and services have in large part had to limit themselves around these systems rather than systems being built around library services and operations.[1] They can best be compared to enterprise resource planning (ERP) systems that are common in corporate or business environments. All ILSs share basic functionality such as circulation control, catalog or inventory, and serials control, but they frequently share other characteristics not exclusive to functionality. They are often robust, complex, rigid, inflexible, expensive, closed, and proprietary in their nature. Sometimes they are best described as "black boxes." In libraries where electronic resources are a bigger part of the picture, vendors have begun offering next-generation ILSs dubbed Library Services Platforms, or LSPs. Even accounting for new functionality relating to e-resource management, for the most part, ILSs have continued to operate and function as they have since the 1990s.[2] When systems exist with little to no change for a prolonged period of time, they become more like a commodity with little differentiation between each system. As in other industries, with commoditization comes opportunities for disruption in the form of OSS.[3] This chapter will provide a brief history and summary of the current state of the ILS, including the appearance of the first OSS ILSs, details on OSS ILSs/LSPs available today, and, finally, a list of vendors that offer support, hosting, and development.

Ralph Halstead Parker is credited with the earliest documented efforts of what would one day be at the core of an ILS. While at the University of Texas at Austin, Parker developed a punch-code system for managing circulation transactions in the 1930s. Later, in 1959, Parker developed another, more sophisticated system for circulation control at the University of Missouri.[4] Other functions or modules that make up a typical ILS are acquisitions, bibliographic/catalog control, serials control, and an online catalog or online public access catalog (OPAC). In 1968, Henriette Avram at the Library of Congress and her team finished initial work on MARC, or MAchine-Readable Cataloging. MARC is the data format that provided a standard for libraries to create and exchange bibliographic information.[5] MARC has also been invaluable in the development of shared bibliographic databases, of which OCLC's WorldCat is probably the most notable example and made possible the adoption of a shared metadata standard across these systems and ILSs.

HISTORY AND CURRENT STATE

Table 3.1. Top 10 globally installed ILSs

ILS	Vendor	United States	Worldwide
Koha	Numerous including standalone	1,086	3,687[b]
Symphony	SirsiDynix	2,565	3,572
Sierra	Innovative Interfaces[a]	1,634	2,148
Alma	Ex Libris[a]	1,065	1,761
Destiny	Follett	1,480	1,530
Polaris	Innovative Interfaces[a]	1,286	1,514
Evergreen	Numerous including standalone	830	943
Atriuum	Book Systems	823	826
Apollo	Biblionix	790	793
Aleph 500	Ex Libris[a]	41	782

Source: "Libraries.org database," Library Technology Guides, accessed March 2–17, 2020, https://library-technology.org/libraries/search.pl.

Note: This data was provided from searching libraries.org database between January and March of 2020.

[a] Ex Libris and Innovative Interfaces are companies/business units of ProQuest.

[b] Global counts for OSS options tend to be underreported. This number could likely be anywhere from 10,000 to 15,000 libraries according to Marshall Breeding in "Open Source Library Systems: The Current State of the Art," Library Technology Reports 53, no. 6 (August 2017): 11 and "Library management," Catalyst, accessed March 20, 2020, https://www.catalyst.net.nz/products/library-management-koha.

An ILS resembles an Enterprise Resource Management (ERM) system that many commercial organizations use to track inventories, payments, and every other conceivable transaction the business performs.[6] The ILS evolved to encompass every operational aspect of managing (until recently) what a library does: acquire, budget for, and manage print-based materials, including describing them via bibliographic control (or cataloging) for allowing them to be found, and, lastly, track the borrowing of the materials to patrons and when they were due back (circulation). The basic architecture of an ILS consists of a database management system to keep track of transactions, relationships, and MARC (and other) bibliographic data and an interface to interact and make changes to that data and the recording of new transactions. While the interface and robustness of the ILS have evolved as computing power has increased and the cost of hardware and software has decreased, the ILS perfectly met the needs of an average library for approximately thirty years without major changes to its overall function.

For any who are curious about the vast amount of merger and acquisition activity of proprietary library software and content companies, Marshall Breeding has made available several eye-opening graphs actively maintained and available at https://librarytechnology.org/mergers/. Based on these graphs, the last twenty or thirty years of merger and acquisition activity beginning in the late 1990s suggests that stability of the overall functionality of the ILS created an environment where ILS vendors could not make any significant inroads into a competitor's market share, so instead, they just bought each other out.

The reason for this may be because the ILS had become in large part what's known as commoditized in that aside from the brand and cost, a customer saw little or no difference between products. In 2004, Andrew Pace likened ILS selection to picking a rental car.[7] As a result, the standardization of functionality meant one vendor's proprietary ILS had little to no competitive advantage over others to convince a library to invest the time and money as well as take on the risk required to migrate from one ILS to another. Adding to that was the fact that each ILS was proprietary from its earliest beginnings and offered little to no integration with other systems. Because of this, libraries increasingly experienced vendor lock-in where libraries felt stuck or at the mercy of the vendor. Vendor lock-in makes for hardly an equitable partnership. For example, a library that was happy with their current system's circulation control but unhappy with the serials control module was stuck with it. It could not use a competitor's serials control without losing interoperability while very likely spending more to support and manage both systems and cover the additional licensing costs. From an overall cost perspective, commoditization generally should drive costs down as "it does not pay to pay more" for a system that has been commoditized, but perhaps as vendor lock-in was very present within the market and was only exacerbated by merger activities, costs did not go down.[8] Indeed, according to Pace, in 2004, many vendors felt libraries weren't paying enough to provide additional development on top of maintenance costs.[9] As a result of the general lack of innovation, costs, commoditization, vendor lock-in, and new software delivery and development methods the Internet made possible, at the turn of the twentieth century, OSS offered libraries the opportunity to innovate and prioritize their system needs with more control at potentially less cost.

OPEN SOURCE OPTIONS

Table 3.2 Open Source ILS and License

OSS ILS	License Type
Koha	GPL—Copyleft
Evergreen	GPL—Copyleft
Invenio	MIT—Permissive
FOLIO	Apache 2.0—Permissive

Koha

Community: https://koha-community.org/
Code: https://github.com/Koha-Community
Live demo: https://koha-community.org/demo/

Koha was the earliest OSS ILS to appear, and while the factors mentioned earlier in this chapter were definitely in play, the need for a system compliant with the date formats of the new millennium, otherwise known as Y2K-complaint, drove its original development. Koha is the first entirely web-based ILS, and it is currently the most popular ILS in the world. It's also unique in that it wasn't originally developed in the United States, and unlike many other ILSs, it has a much smaller US footprint in proportion to its overall use. Koha was originally developed in 1999 by Kapito Communications for the Horowhenua Library Trust, or HLT, in New Zealand. While Marshall Breeding's librarytechnology.org database has approximately 4,000 libraries worldwide as of this writing,[10] an ALA Library Technology Report authored by Breeding in 2017 reported 4,500 and that the true number very likely exceeds 10,000 due to underreporting in developing countries.[11] Catalyst, a service provider to Koha, states it may be over 15,000.[12] The story of Koha's adoption is not only a highlight of OSS in libraries, but it is also one in the general OSS world. The service providers around the world and the community that has grown up around it is impressive. Koha means gift in Māori.

Koha

Can you share the story of Koha at your organization?
My university was the first to go live with Koha in 2010. They decided to consider open source solutions after a poor experience with a call for tender where they chose a commercial solution: Just after the decision, the software company merged with another one and decided to stop the maintenance on the ILS they had chosen. In 2010, we needed a lot of local developments because few universities went live with Koha then. But, year after year, almost all the local developments have been integrated in Koha or other permitting the same enhancements.

How would you describe the Koha community?
The Koha community is a very welcoming open source community. Everyone involved is enthusiastic when a new library installed Koha. There are people from each continent, and they are all working together to get Koha better. The mailing list and the chat are really active, and you could be helped if need. The different companies are working together; there [is more] cooperation than competition. As I'm at the head of the French Koha user groups, I was able to meet a lot of Koha users or workers during conferences or Hackfest; these meetings were stimulating for all involved.

How has Koha benefitted your organization?
First, Koha is evolving each year, and we can benefit from new enhancements to provide new services. Next year, for example, we want to use the new ILL module to manage it in Koha rather than in spreadsheet files. Second, as we have a technical colleague in the team, we can do other enhancements, and we can provide services closer to our needs. A few years ago, there was a discussion about merging with other universities, and a collective reflection took place to know what were our assets, and most of our colleagues said, "Koha!"

Sonia Bouis
Université Jean Moulin Lyon 3
Lyon, France

Background and Current State

In 1999, the HLT, a group consisting of three libraries serving a total of 30,000 people on the north island of New Zealand, put out a Request for Proposals, or RFP, for a new ILS that was Y2K-compliant and could be accessed over a dial-up internet connection. There were no responses. HLT and Kapito Communications, a software company, then looked for an OSS ILS to customize and implement. There were none. Work began on Koha in September 1999. By January 3, 2000, Koha was live. Though the original version of Koha lacked many aspects crucial to modern libraries, including support for MARC, in regard to Y2K compliance, the deadline was quite immutable. The fact that the most popular ILS in the world was initially developed in three months is incredible and perhaps indicative of just how commoditized ILSs had become. HLT's and Kapito's efforts didn't go unnoticed. By January 2001, Koha version 1 was published on sourceforge.net for download, received its first translation request (Polish), was awarded the 3M Innovation in Libraries Award, and had 874 commits to its code.[13] By November 2001, Koha was using the Z39.50 protocol and able to import MARC records.

Koha is built on a LAMP stack with Linux, often Debian-based distributions, Apache, MySQL (increasingly MariaDB), and Perl. While some may be surprised that the system is written in Perl, as Casey Bisson in 2007 wrote in an ALA Library Technology Report titled "Open-Source Software For Libraries," "Perl, a language that served both the developers and the user community in two significant ways: Perl is common and well supported on almost all Unix or Linux operating systems, allowing software written in Perl to run on a huge variety of systems with no additional effort from the developer," and "Perl applications are compiled at run time, requiring that they be distributed in source-code form, not as an opaque and inscrutable binary."[14] Though Perl is less popular today, especially on such a large scale, it is still widely available, accessible, and, for a developer, has a low barrier to entry in using. As of this writing, over 400 individual developers have pushed changes to the codebase of Koha, and the latest general release version is version 20. This international and diverse group of developers represents the international user community and may well represent the ideal organic OSS community.

Outside of developer communication channels, Koha as a software project is loosely governed by a committee formed by Horowhenua Library Trust.[15] The public and staff interfaces of Koha have been translated into over forty languages.

While the story and success of Koha is an international one, it had early and important developments in the United States. The director of the first, if not one of the first, libraries in the United States to express interest in adopting Koha contacted the Koha listserv in January 2002. Stephen Hedges at Nelsonville Public Library, or NPL, in Athens County, Ohio, was using a legacy ILS with limited support available in North America. Instead of migrating to another proprietary ILS, they put $10,000 towards additional development to support MARC 21 formats, Z39.50, NCIP, and SIP2 to stay in line with national standards, to participate in statewide lending programs, and to continue their self-checkout services, respectively, for the community of approximately 60,000 they supported. These enhancements improved Koha's interoperability with other library systems, thereby making it easier for libraries to migrate to the OSS ILS. As a result, these changes made Koha that much more appealing to libraries tired of high costs and vendor lock-in. NPL went live in August 2003. The systems administrator at NPL, Joshua Ferraro, would go on to found one of the first service providers dedicated to Koha, known as LibLime, in March 2005.

The development NPL sponsored would be continued by other libraries adopting Koha and sculpting it to their needs while sharing the new features with the entire community. This trend continues today and indeed is a requirement of the copyleft license Koha's source code uses. Some organizations fund their own development or outsource to service providers. As crowdsource funding has grown in popularity, it has been adopted by the Koha community as a way to not only make active development and improvement more affordable but also helps to prioritize development of enhancements and new features. Another important enhancement was the addition of IndexData's Zebra indexing and retrieval engine funded by the Crawford County Federated Library System in Pennsylvania.[16] This allowed larger libraries to run Koha without the risk of overburdening MySQL, which can experience performance issues with heavier traffic and querying. In 2019, the popular, enterprise-quality index engine Elasticsearch was officially made available as an alternative to Zebra to support larger instances of Koha.[17]

Community and Service Providers

Service providers offer support in hosting, migration, development, and much of the organizational leadership and overall shape of Koha. The success and cooperation of these providers, in no small part, has aided in the success of Koha itself. While there are several service providers, most specialize or limit their customer base to a specific region of the globe. The following service providers make up the bulk of current hosting and support options:

BibLibre (https://www.biblibre.com/en/): Based in France and founded in 2007, BibLibre is a formalization of consulting and contract development work done by several individuals in regards to Koha, specifically, Paul

Poulain, who started doing development work for Koha in 2002 working on the initial MARC and the translation tool.[18] They have support contracts with over 170 libraries—mostly in France—based on libraries.org data.[19]

ByWater Solutions (https://bywatersolutions.com/): LibLime's missteps (see LibLime/PTFS section for more detail) allowed other service providers in the United States to gain a foothold as alternatives better aligned with the Koha Community.[20] ByWater Solutions, founded in 2009, is now the premier service provider of Koha to libraries in the United States and Canada, with over 900 service contracts in North America. These contracts make up the majority of all Koha installations in the United States and Canada.[21] ByWater Solutions has been instrumental in making Koha more appealing to academic libraries in the United States. In cooperation with EBSCO, ByWater Solutions developed an integration with Koha's native OPAC and EBSCO's discovery service, EDS, assisted in the development of making Elasticsearch, an index search and retrieval option to support large library catalogs, and worked on integration with the OSS electronic resource management system, or ERMS, CORAL. Much of this development is done on behalf of libraries they provide services to and are done in collaboration with the Koha community and other service providers.

Catalyst (https://www.catalyst.net.nz/): Catalyst is an IT software development and consulting firm headquartered in Wellington, New Zealand, and it has been focused on OSS software solutions for a range of industries. As with most of the service providers described in this section, they offer hosting, migration, and support, and they are actively involved in the development of Koha. In early 2020, Catalyst acquired Calyx Information Essentials, a major service provider for Koha in Australia.[22] Based on data from libraries.org, Calyx manages twenty-seven Koha libraries in Australia, more than doubling Catalyst's Koha contracts in Australia and New Zealand to approximately forty-five.[23]

Equinox (https://www.equinoxinitiative.org/): Born from and made up of the developers who created the Evergreen ILS, the Equinox Open Library Initiative was originally founded in 2007. While they specialize in support, hosting, and development for Evergreen, they offer the same services for Koha as well. Unique to Equinox is the Sequoia service they have developed, allowing for quick deployment and scalability of various systems.[24] Based on libraries.org data, a total of thirty-two libraries in the United States and Canada contract with them for Koha services.[25]

Interleaf Technology (https://www.interleaf.ie): Supporting libraries mostly in Ireland, but also in Germany and Austria, based on libraries.org data, Interleaf has been around since 1998 and is based in Bray, Ireland, a coastal town just south of Dublin. A libraries.org search has a count of twenty-eight libraries contracting with Interleaf for Koha support while the Interleaf website lists ninety libraries as partners in Ireland alone.[26]

LibLime/PTFS (https://koha.org/): Founded in 2005 by Joshua Ferraro previously at NPL, LibLime promised a bright future for Koha in the United States. They completed the work to incorporate Zebra as part of Koha's search and retrieval, and in 2007, they acquired the koha.org domain name, Koha copyrights, documentation, active service contracts, and employees working on the Koha project from Kapito Communications. Their executive management team also consisted of veterans from many proprietary library automation companies.[27] Perhaps, in this case, that was a weakness rather than a strength. In 2009, LibLime embarked on a fork of Koha, intending it to appeal to larger libraries. The company's leadership would dub the fork LibLime Enterprise Koha. It would include applications separate from Koha's codebase, including closed-source applications. This would be a separate development project from Koha and solely conducted by LibLime. This move, however well-intended, was not well-received by the Koha community, including many of LibLime's customers, and disrupted the spirit of cooperation that is essential for successful OSS projects. To exacerbate the issue, the koha.org domain, copyrights, and documentation were now owned by an organization not aligned with the overall Koha community.

In 2010, LibLime was acquired by PTFS, a US-based service provider with a track record of catering to libraries associated with the US Federal Government and its agencies. The acquisition included the Koha assets, including the koha.org domain. PTFS continues to develop their fork of Koha separately from the original source code. Based on data from libraries.org, they manage 128 Koha libraries in the United States and Canada. LibLime's involvement with the Koha project and community is an important one for the history of Koha in the United States, prospective users of Koha, as well as any prospective user of OSS. LibLime's story should also serve as an important lesson to service providers on the importance of community. As the saying goes, "If you want to go fast, go alone; but if you want to go far, go together."

PTFS Europe Limited (https://www.ptfs-europe.com/): Operating independently of the US-based PTFS, PTFS Europe offers an array of Library OSS options, including the main version of Koha as opposed to LibLime Koha. Within the United Kingdom, based on libraries.org data, they have support and hosting agreements with over 110 libraries.[28]

As already noted, Koha's community is international and diverse. Though the major development efforts have continued to follow other popular OSS systems with a concentration of individuals and service providers being from developed countries like the United States, the United Kingdom and Commonwealth countries, and members of the European Union, Koha's architecture and governing structure make it fairly easy for libraries, individuals, or start-up service providers to get involved in the main project or to create their own fork of Koha. For example, the largest known instance of Koha is in Turkey, where the Devinim Software company runs their own Koha version to integrate every public library in Turkey, a total of over 1,300 libraries, two million users, and seventeen million items.[29]

Future Outlook

While the majority of libraries that have used Koha have been small to medium public libraries, the limitations of Koha and, perhaps more importantly, the historic perceptions of Koha have continued to be challenged with every major release. Increasingly, in the United States, larger public and academic libraries have begun adopting Koha. There could be a few reasons for this. Interest in OSS has only increased in the last five to ten years. Mergers and acquisitions of library vendors are ongoing, and traditional proprietary ILSs have failed to innovate with the exceptions of vertical integration (a whole new level of vendor lock-in) and SaaS-based LSPs, or Library Services Platforms, which are either cost-prohibitive and/or developed with a small section of the market in mind (e.g., academic and research libraries typically on the large side). In 2018, Virginia Polytechnic Institute and State University, commonly known as Virginia Tech, went live with Koha. Holding around two million bibliographic records serving approximately 35,000 students, this is the largest academic library system to date to implement Koha. On the public library side, there are more than a dozen libraries, mostly in the United States and United Kingdom, that serve populations greater than 200,000 using Koha as their ILS.[30] Koha's release schedule shows no signs of slowing down. Adoption of Koha in both developing and developed countries has been increasing over the last several years, and the Koha community and partnerships with other OSS and proprietary applications remains strong. As larger and better-funded libraries become involved, the benefits should continue to expand for libraries in developing countries where Koha remains the most accessible ILS.

Evergreen

    Community: https://evergreen-ils.org
    Code: https://github.com/evergreen-library-system
    Live demo: https://wiki.evergreen-ils.org/doku.php?id=community_servers

The Evergreen project was initiated in June 2004 by the Georgia State Library System (GPLS) for their PINES consortium to replace a costly, poor-performing, and proprietary-shared ILS and Catalog experience used

Evergreen

Can you share the story of Evergreen at your organization?
Ann Arbor District Library (AADL) planned its migration to Evergreen over the course of years. In 2018, we brought these plans to fruition in tandem with the launch of a new website. Our website catalog integrated with Evergreen records and allowed us easier control over functionality and data. Since then, we have brought numerous features to our staff and users due to Evergreen's open database access and the ability to quickly tie in various software with OpenSRF calls. Evergreen has greatly increased the user experience for everyone involved, and AADL is always making improvements thanks to Evergreen's open source nature.

How would you describe the Evergreen community?
The Evergreen community is wonderfully welcoming. There are many people who have been involved since the beginning, but they are always open to new people coming in to learn. If you ever have a question, there are multiple ways to reach out. Many members of the community will often come together to help figure out a solution or plan new ideas. The Evergreen IRC channel has always been a terrific place, whether to chat or ask questions.

How has Evergreen benefitted your organization?
Evergreen has been a tremendous boon to AADL. Because we are able to dig into source code and have open access to the database, AADL has been able to build numerous tools to help both users and staff. We have a custom-built API that can integrate Evergreen data with a number of services. This allowed us to craft an improved aadl.org experience with much higher responsiveness on actions, as well as new features. We were able to build a tool to let staff check out holds to users without even bringing up Evergreen, as another example. Evergreen continually improves, and we expect our appreciation for it will continue to grow as well!

Troy Leonard
Ann Arbor District Library
Ann Arbor, Michigan, USA

by nearly every public library in the state.[31] From 2004 to 2006, Evergreen was developed to support the consortium's 250 member libraries, eight million items, and over one and a half million patrons. It went live in September 2006. Built for a consortium with many different tiers and many different-sized libraries, Evergreen is well-suited for consortia and has been adopted by many in the United States and Canada. Today, there are nearly 1,000 libraries using Evergreen, making it one of the most popular ILSs in the world.[32]

Background and Current State

Licensed under a GNU GPL license, Evergreen's codebase is copyleft. Designed to support millions of items and patrons, it is a very robust system relying on the scalability of the PostgreSQL relational database management system and OpenSRF, or Open Scalable Request Framework. This framework was developed specifically for Evergreen to handle a large number of transactions at once, as would be expected in a consortia or library network environment. Like Koha, it is using Perl in addition to C. The system relies on Apache for its web services and Linux as an OS. Original versions of Evergreen relied on a staff-client application like many legacy ILSs. Unlike Koha, Evergreen was developed in-house by GPLS. After the successful launch of the initial version of Evergreen, similar libraries were interested in using Evergreen. In response, the development team at GPLS formed Equinox Software in 2007, becoming Equinox Open Library Initiative in 2017, to provide hosting, development, and support for Evergreen libraries, including those in the PINES consortium.

Like Koha, Evergreen has been consistently enhanced and supports all expected protocols a modern library system is expected to need. Like most ILSs, rather than LSPs, Evergreen excels at print management-related tasks and workflows. While originally reliant on an installed client application on each staff workstation, starting with version 3.0 and later, the staff client has been phased out by a browser-based staff application increasingly expected with modern ILSs and LSPs. For school and consortia library systems, not having to troubleshoot issues related to the client and often a specific workstation mitigates many issues that a staff user might experience where IT personnel may not be on-site and therefore cannot quickly address the issue. Additionally, browser-based clients often translate to an OS-agnostic ILS in that a staff user's workstation doesn't require a specific operating system such as Windows, and the specific hardware requirements of the workstation to use the ILS are lessened.

In 2009, one of the busiest library systems in the United States migrated to Evergreen, marking a significant achievement for Evergreen and OSS in libraries. King County Library System, or KCLS, in Washington State regularly processes over twenty-one million checkout transactions at its fifty libraries.[33] KCLS, along with libraries in Michigan, California, and Florida, secured an IMLS one-million-dollar grant to adopt Evergreen. KCLS contributed one million dollars of their own funds to match grant funding for Evergreen development, documentation, and migration.[34] KCLS was able to "experiment with, and then migrate to, the OSS Evergreen ILS," as Matt Enis put it in a 2013 *Library Journal* article.[35]

While Evergreen was built for large and complex systems, it perhaps wasn't tuned for such an active library with so many annual transactions as reports of patrons not being able to pay fines, slow searches on the catalog, and other issues dogged what should have been a major celebration for the KCLS and OSS advocates in libraries.[36] In response, KCLS put out an RFP calling for assistance, illustrating one of the main advantages of OSS software, which is freedom to move from one service provider to another or even doing it yourself. A company, at the time called Catalyst IT Services (not related to the New Zealand company of the same name), was awarded the contract, and they aggressively, along with Command Prompt, Inc., a company specializing in PostgreSQL databases, started to develop and support KCLS's Evergreen instance.[37] Catalyst was able to prioritize and correct issues at a speed that no proprietary company or service provider could match, which KCLS's size ultimately required. This move has resulted in KCLS's Evergreen ILS being so different from the original Evergreen project that it is now considered a fork of Evergreen. While this development was slightly similar to LibLime's efforts to develop an enterprise quality system separate from the original Koha project, KCLS's situation was untenable as the restraints of Evergreen were crippling KCLS's operations, and no other Evergreen libraries or Evergreen community assets were directly impacted by these moves. It's unfortunate KCLS was unable to identify the issues before going to production and lacked the needed time to work with the Evergreen community to address and ultimately share the improvements as part of the main Evergreen project. If they had, perhaps other large, often cost-strapped, urban library systems would be using Evergreen today, redirecting hundreds of thousands, sometimes millions, of dollars worth of funds spent on library systems for more library resources or, worst case, Evergreen-related administration or development roles creating job opportunities in the communities they serve.

Unlike certain assets of Koha being owned by its original developer and then acquired by another company, in Evergreen's case, the University

System of Georgia, of which the GPLS is a part, retained the rights for the Evergreen trademark and other copyrightable assets instead of going with the developers who formed Equinox. In 2012, Evergreen joined the Software Freedom Conservancy, which provides administrative and financial expertise for OSS projects.[38] With this change came the creation of a governing Evergreen Oversight Board and the Evergreen project's trademark being transferred to the Software Freedom Conservancy.[39] In April 2019, the community elected a project board as part of an effort to transition to a stand-alone nonprofit 501(c)(3) organization.[40]

Community and Service Providers

Service providers offer support in hosting, migration, and development, but the overall development path is managed by Evergreen's Oversight Board. This board primarily consists of representatives from library networks and consortia rather than service providers. While there are some international Evergreen libraries, the vast majority of libraries are based in the United States and Canada. There are also fewer service providers, and much of the expertise regarding Evergreen's development is based at Equinox. The following service providers make up the current hosting, support, and custom development options:

Catalyte (https://catalyte.io/): Not related to the company based in New Zealand that offers Koha support, Catalyst IT Services has since rebranded to become Catalyte, offering a range of services from Agile project management services, software-developer apprenticeships, software-developer staffing for projects, employee reskilling, and technology consulting and services for organizations shifting their business objectives and strategy. While they appear to still provide support and development to KCPL, they do not actively advertise their services or market to other libraries.[41] Any library that might approach Catalyte regarding Evergreen would need to keep in mind that KCPL's Evergreen is a forked version of the main Evergreen community project. Since they now are no stranger to library systems, it will be interesting to see how this relationship to the industry evolves over time, especially if other libraries or OSS communities approach them on future project needs.

Equinox (https://www.equinoxinitiative.org/): As mentioned previously in this chapter, Equinox was founded by the original development team at GPLS as Equinox Software in 2007; it is now a 501(c)(3) nonprofit formally called Equinox Open Library Initiative providing the range of service provider options for Koha, Evergreen, and an OSS interlibrary loan (ILL) application called FulfILLment. Perhaps in response to KCLS moving away from Equinox's support in 2014, Equinox made available Sequoia, a hosting platform supporting multi-tenant functionality opening up capacity and instances for services they support. With contract agreements with around 500 libraries, it accounts for half of all Evergreen installs in the libraries.org database.[42]

Emerald Data Networks (http://www.emeralddata.net/): Based in Atlanta, Georgia, Emerald Data Networks provides IT services in a range of industries. They provide support, data migration, and hosting services. Based on libraries.org data, they provide services for approximately ten libraries in Texas.[43]

MOBIUS (https://mobiusconsortium.org): MOBIUS was founded in 1998 as part of the University of Missouri System, but since 2010, it has operated as an independent 501(3)(c) nonprofit. It began as a consortium for Missouri but now includes members from other states and offers a range of services, including hosting and support for Evergreen. The service is called MOSS or MOBIUS Open Source Solutions. They provide services for forty-seven libraries, all of which are located in North Carolina, according to the libraries.org database.[44]

Future Outlook

Evergreen's robustness and complexity have impacted and guided its adoption and international reach. For small library systems or in developing countries where there may be less expertise available, Evergreen can be more difficult to adopt and manage, especially when compared to Koha's lighter footprint and that project's early language translation work and documentation. However, as developing countries begin to invest more heavily in libraries, there will likely be more interest and available expertise to take advantage of Evergreen's great strength at managing large library networks. In developed parts of the world, KCPL's success makes it clear Evergreen can support large and very active library systems. However, to do this, libraries might need to deviate from the original Evergreen project unless they have the time and patience to work within the community to develop enhancements as part of the official project.

Invenio

Community: https://invenio-software.org/products/ils/
Code: https://github.com/inveniosoftware/invenio-app-ils
Live Demo: none found, but https://invenio-software.org/showcase/ has examples of sites using various components of Invenio, including TIND sites.

Originally created as a digital repository and ILS known as CDSWare in 2002, Invenio was created by the folks at CERN.[45] CERN is the European Laboratory for Particle Physics, home of the Large Hadron Collider and where Tim Berners-Lee worked when he invented the World Wide Web in 1989.[46] Just as the World Wide Web was originally created for sharing information with researchers and scholars, Invenio was created by the folks at CERN for storing and sharing research. As will be discussed in chapter 4, systems for storing research data, pre-prints, scholarly articles, and digital objects has been a fast-growing niche of library systems as libraries shift focus to digital scholarship and publishing, so it is no surprise that CERN would have the same needs and use their expertise to design their own. With a modern and flexible architecture, version 3 of the Invenio framework the ILS is built upon has much to offer libraries that are perhaps looking for something more modern than a traditional ILS without committing to high cost and multiple module aspects of an LSP.

Background and Current State

While the original Invenio version 1, or CDSWare, was a software application "that acted as both a digital repository and an integrated library system based on MARC21," version 3 is a complete rewrite designed to be mostly metadata agnostic and make use of modern, OSS architectures. Version 3 broke the repository, digital management, and ILS into modules that sit on top of the framework dubbed Invenio Version 3.[47] Version 3 is built on Python, Elasticsearch, originally MySQL, but it can now support PostgreSQL and NoSQL type databases with Linux as the OS these components are installed on. It is quite powerful and robust, and the UI is a bit nontraditional as there is only one interface for staff and users and what a user has access to is entirely based on roles they are assigned. This is quite a refreshing approach.

Though originally released under a GPL copyleft license, it has recently been converted to a permissive MIT license.[48] This might have been done to accommodate an official CERN spin-off, TIND, whose developers have since forked Invenio to create proprietary systems based on Invenio's version 3 platform. TIND has made significant inroads in marketing Invenio-based TIND modules with academic libraries such as Caltech and UC Berkeley Law adopting TIND's ILS as well as improvements on the development of the ILS that originally lacked important acquisitions and serials components. TIND's fork of Invenio may still be compatible to the extent that the developments they make are pushed to the OSS Invenio project. However, as a proprietary licensed software application, they are not required to share its code with CERN unless a separate agreement exists outside the scope of software licensing. What makes this even more interesting in that part of TIND's brand is that they're based on an OSS system built at CERN.[49] Though some might feel this is a misleading marketing tactic since TIND is not available under an OSS license, it demonstrates how far OSS has come. Proprietary software companies are now using a product's OSS history as a selling point.

Community and Service Providers

Invenio's community might be best described as a niche not deviating outside of scientific and research libraries, even though TIND is making inroads in the United States with more diverse organizations. It appears Invenio's most prominent user is CERN itself when not factoring in TIND installs, but it's clear through TIND that the Invenio platform is capable of supporting medium and large academic and research libraries. TIND's presence in the market will continue to grow. Invenio's governing body is CERN itself, but this may be changing, as noted on Invenio's official website.[50] As of this writing, there appear to be no service providers for the OSS Invenio ILS component.

Future Outlook

The platform Invenio ILS sits upon is modern, scalable, and OSS at heart, but its success in more and larger libraries (outside of proprietary vendors who fork it) depends on whether a community and the necessary service providers can grow around it and ideally as organically as possible. This appears to be happening to other components of Invenio like the Research Data Management module, or RDM, but it will take at least one high visibility library or established OSS service provider to make it a viable option in today's ILS environment. However, those libraries and service providers might have little reason to do this with the other OSS ILS alternatives available.

FOLIO

> Community: https://www.folio.org/
> Code: https://dev.folio.org/source-code/
> Live Demo: https://wiki.folio.org/ under "Demo Sites" heading for all available options.

The FOLIO project represents a watershed moment in the history of libraries and their relationship with OSS software. FOLIO stands for the "Future of Libraries Is Open." Begun in 2015, FOLIO is a multi-tenant LSP designed with the potential to support large academic and research libraries. While still in development, several libraries around the world have gone live with all or parts of FOLIO. With several organizations, including library vendors, software developers, and large academic libraries in the United States actively participating in the governance, development, and management of the FOLIO project, FOLIO has generated a lot of interest in the library profession. From a technical perspective, FOLIO's architecture combined with its permissive

FOLIO

Can you share the story of FOLIO at your organization?
In 2017, we were in the process of looking for a new library system and chose to work together with EBSCO as their beta test partner in developing a new open source LSP. The thought of open source and, for real, being able to influence our new system was very tempting while at the same time we wanted to be customers and get hosting and support from an established company. So that was the beginning of our FOLIO journey, starting off with a paper product and going live two years later as the first FOLIO library in the world. Our goal was to have an easy-to-use system where we could choose the functions we needed.

How would you describe the FOLIO community?
One tipping point for us in adopting a new system was being part of a community where we could learn from each other. The FOLIO community is a vibrant, hardworking source of energy and ambition. A cornucopia of nice, knowledgeable, and helpful people belonging to both commercial companies and independent institutions.

How has FOLIO benefitted your organization?
Being part of the development of a brand-new library system with less mature or different functionality has been a great opportunity to reevaluate how we do things and what functions that are most important. Integrating management of electronic resources into the LSP was very important for us, and FOLIO has proven to be a flexible and efficient ERM system. It has been a great learning experience, both for our FOLIO team but also for all colleagues that were involved along the way.

Marie Widigson and Marie Wenander
Chalmers University of Technology
Gothenburg, Sweden

OSS license has the potential to completely transform the library systems environment on a scale not seen since the earliest library automation and networked databases became mainstream. Just as early automation systems helped to define libraries in the latter half of the twentieth century, FOLIO may come to define them in the first half of the twenty-first century.[51]

Background and Current State

There are multiple factors involved in the appearance of the FOLIO project and its already moderately sized community, generous funding, and early success. While not the first, an early sponsor was OLE, or Open Library Environment. OLE began as the Open Library Environment Project in 2008, funded by the Mellon Foundation to a tune of over $6 million to participating universities to create a next-generation library system.[52] Its members consisted of mostly large academic libraries. The project group partnered with Kuali Foundation and was intended to be an OSS development project. Through a combination of Kuali shifting from a nonprofit to a commercial business, and a limitation that could not be overcome in Kuali's Rice middleware, the project foundered, and though some libraries implemented parts of Kuali OLE, it never came to fruition.[53] In 2016, those still interested in pursuing a next-generation OSS library system had become involved as full partners and collaborators in the FOLIO project with no trace of the former Kuali OLE project on the OLE website.[54]

EBSCO, the original initiator of the FOLIO project, may surprise some, but EBSCO has been actively working with OSS integration and partnering with OSS service providers for some time. Most notable has been the company's partnership with ByWater Solutions to integrate EBSCO's EDS discovery service with Koha. While any integration work done requires time and money, EBSCO's strategy has appeared to be that they stay focused on their specialty in the industry, which is content rather than building their own systems. This strategy is less costly and less risky than developing their own proprietary system, which would invariably make it harder to integrate their products with other proprietary systems as they become more competitive and less collaborative with each other. This strategy also has the benefit of potentially disrupting their largest competitor, ProQuest, which has taken a different strategic path that some might describe as vertical integration by not only acquiring Serials Solutions, an early innovator in e-resource management, in 2004, but also the maker of the LSP Alma, Ex Libris, in 2015, and most recently, in December 2019, acquiring one of the oldest and largest library systems companies, Innovate Interfaces, Inc. The same year ProQuest acquired ExLibris is also the year the FOLIO project was initiated by EBSCO. If successful, FOLIO will offer the best alternative to Alma and its ProQuest-centric platform. Some might argue OCLC's WMS LSP is a currently available alternative to Alma, but there has been a significant slowdown in WMS implementations and adoptions and a steady decline in member satisfaction with WMS.[55] Perhaps most notably, very few ARLs and large academic libraries have adopted WMS even compared to early FOLIO adopters.[56]

Another major factor in the FOLIO project has been the software development leadership provided by IndexData.[57] Though many of their employees are based in the United States, IndexData has historically been a Europe-based organization and is still able to boast about an international team. They've also helped to build the more international segment of the blossoming FOLIO community. No stranger to library systems and OSS projects, IndexData has consistently blazed a trail in the industry; their YAZ and Zebra applications stand as solid examples.[58] EBSCO partnered with IndexData fairly early in the process. Though a small organization, their presence in gathering requirements for the project, talking about the long-term vision and possibilities of the system, and project outreach at conferences and special events has had a huge impact on awareness of FOLIO that cannot be overstated. They are the lead developers and architects for the FOLIO project.

While FOLIO can be described as a multi-tenant LSP (like Alma and WMS), its architecture is quite a departure from other library systems. FOLIO has been described as APIs, or Application Programming Interfaces, all the way down.[59] For example, instead of traditional ILS modules such as a circulation area that contains many functions and features like patron lookup, fines management, notices, and checkout and check-in of materials, FOLIO instead relies on microservices where each of these functions would exist on their own and be able to fully interact with other microservices where necessary. This is an increasingly popular method to build scalable applications.[60] This model most resembles an operating system where applications are installed on top of a platform or kernel that requires those applications to conform to a set of established standards and, to an extent, guarantees interoperability. A common example used is the modern smartphone, its OS, and its marketplace for supplemental applications. A device originally intended to be just a phone is suddenly much more with many small and basic applications pre-installed that make daily life easier, but it's also able to be customized to serve any type of industry or any type of individual's needs. If successful, the FOLIO project could very well create a paradigm shift in libraries and other cultural organizations, and it could open up the types of systems and services these organizations can make available to their communities.

As far as technical specifics, at FOLIO's lowest level is the system layer, which encompasses the database or databases, storage aspects, and indexing aspects. The intent of FOLIO is to operate in a way as to never be overcommitted to a specific technology. For example, the earliest iterations of FOLIO were originally designed to work with MongoDB, but PostgreSQL was found to better accommodate some of the requirements of library applications.[61] Between this layer and the application layer is the Okapi layer, described as a microservices API gateway for passing data back and forth between the system and application layers.[62] The application layer is where the microservice applications live, and above that is the user-interface layer. This layer, dubbed Stripes, is responsible for establishing standardized layouts to create a consistent appearance and user experience within FOLIO. It utilizes the React JavaScript library. Okapi and Stripes are referred to as the Okapi-Stripes platform, and it is fully multi-tenant.

FOLIO is licensed under the permissive Apache 2 license that allows modification and distribution and also allows for commercial purposes as well. Unlike say the Linux kernel, that is licensed under GPL version 2, the Apache 2 license will allow any company to use the source code of FOLIO and build an application on top of it that is closed source and proprietary. Ironically, the more successful the platform is, the more likely we'll see that happen, as we have seen with every core OSS application such as the application the Apache 2 license is named for. We could see many proprietary library systems companies build their own next-generation systems on top of the FOLIO core code in the same manner that much proprietary software is built using open-core applications like Apache, PostgreSQL, Java, PHP, etc. That's not necessarily a bad thing, as OSS core applications often have the largest market share in their respective niche and huge communities built around them, ensuring the support, sustainability, and security are in place to continue to be successfully used by any and all interested. If this comes to pass, the type of foundational standard that appears could have a huge impact on library systems development, standards, and even extend to the ability to standardize training for library personnel, eliminating barriers currently in existence due to proprietary systems.[63]

The 501(c)(3) nonprofit OLF, or Open Library Foundation, created in 2016 and briefly discussed in chapter 2, was created to support two pre-existing OSS projects: The Open Library Environment (OLE) and the Global Open Knowledgebase (GOKb). Along with FOLIO, it includes other similarly aligned OSS projects, including other projects we'll cover in this guide, such as ReShare, VuFind, and CORAL. Its membership consists of individuals, institutions, organizations, and commercial vendors and service providers. Additionally, the OLF hosts WOLFcon for its members and those interested in meeting and discussing its various projects. Similar to the Software Freedom Conservancy, the OLF is able to provide organizational expertise and administrative assistance to its member projects. Based on libraries.org data, there are already twenty-six libraries using some element of FOLIO.[64]

Community and Service Providers

Though still in the early stages of the FOLIO project, the community is growing in international membership, especially in Europe, but also in Asia, with the Shanghai Library System work on implementing FOLIO.[65] Its US-based community consists mostly of large research and academic libraries with resources to devote to development, project management, systems analysis and design, and to serve as SMEs, or Subject Matter Experts, in their domain area. The results of all of this work have shaped FOLIO's overall design. This should bode well for many academic libraries who have similar workflows and needs. How well this translates to public libraries is questionable. As with all other LSPs, the emphasis of functionality and development has been on electronic resources that make up the bulk of the average academic library's collection, but public libraries are still dominated by print and prioritize print management functionality over e-resource management if they are using an ERM at all. However, FOLIO is designed in a way that as other stakeholders from different types of libraries become involved, any functionality needs should be easy to address one microservice at a time. Overall, the community is very much academic library-based, but if FOLIO is successful, we should expect that to change. The following service providers plan to or already are hosting and supporting FOLIO:

ByWater Solutions (https://bywatersolutions.com): No stranger to OSS library systems and a solid track record of being a good OSS community member, ByWater Solutions has several contracts in place to provide support and hosting of FOLIO that are not yet live as of this writing. As much of their current client base is small to medium public and academic libraries, FOLIO should offer ByWater a path to larger academic library partners and eventually the larger public library market still dominated by proprietary vendors. Consistently praised for their high customer service ratings, they should be an appealing option to many of their current client base and other small to medium libraries looking to migrate to FOLIO, especially if those libraries have a smaller technology and systems footprint or if they will benefit from assistance with change management and hands-on training.[66]

EBSCO (https://www.ebsco.com/products/ebsco-folio-library-services): Though EBSCO is one of the largest companies in the library market, FOLIO represents a new line of business for EBSCO, providing migration, support, hosting, and continual support for FOLIO as well as ensuring its other products integrate as well as possible with it. They have a number of contracts already, including University of Alabama, Missouri State University, and the first library in the world to go live (October 2019) with FOLIO, Chalmers University of Technology in Sweden. Their stake in the FOLIO project has dictated the earliest integration options being tied to current EBSCO products such as EDS and E-Holdings. As a result, with lots of community participation, they now have in their hands on an LSP that rivals Alma. If they continue to actively participate in the community and work to ensure other integrations are successful, it will continue to be a win for EBSCO, a win for the FOLIO community, a win for OSS in libraries, and a win for the entire library landscape.

IndexData (https://www.indexdata.com/folio/): IndexData also has a few high-profile contracts for FOLIO, including Duke and Lehigh Universities.[67] As the lead architect and developer for the project, many libraries will be interested in contracting IndexData's support and hosting services, which will no doubt be supplemented by IndexData's in-depth knowledge and experience with FOLIO already. However, like EBSCO, this will be IndexData's first foray into becoming a service provider. What IndexData lacks in migration and customer support experience, they may be able to quickly make up for by being better able to develop tools to assist with the service provider aspects of the business.

This list could quickly expand based on how successful early implementer libraries are with FOLIO. SirsiDynix, a major provider of proprietary library systems, as table 3.1 illustrates, has expressed interest in becoming a service provider as far back as 2016.[68] If they or other proprietary vendors become more involved with FOLIO, this could mark a sweeping transition from continuing development of their current systems to dedicated support, hosting, and development of FOLIO's OSS platform or ensuring their close-source products can easily integrate with FOLIO apps or function as apps within FOLIO itself. Aside from the largest, well-staffed libraries, unlike Koha and Evergreen, there will likely be few libraries able to successfully host FOLIO themselves as FOLIO's architecture is more resource-intensive and not easily hosted on just one server, though hosting through an IaaS provider like AWS or Azure could be a viable path to self-hosting.

Future Outlook

How successful the marketplace is within FOLIO will define the extent of its future success. Those commoditized functions of an ILS, like most circulation functions, will be easy to customize and hard to charge for, but for the new and innovative services that could serve specific types of cultural organizations from small public libraries to large academic to museums or archives, we might see something else. These could be available for a fee, or maybe free to install, but services available in it are only available with a license or subscription akin to in-app purchases business models used for many smartphone applications. For those commoditized services, who will be responsible for maintenance and support? Will users be just as locked-in as they were previously, but something that looks more like a modern-day cable subscription where you can pick a designated configuration or flavor? As FOLIO's underlying architecture will be too advanced for many libraries to host their own instance, hosting will likely increasingly continue to be available as a service instead, but what will happen to support aspects? Could we see a shift of support and development roles back into libraries as these types of roles in general become more in-demand and popular career choices? In the end, if the marketplace is successful, we should expect to see FOLIO become a basic foundation of library systems not too dissimilar from how operating systems on servers, PCs, and mobile devices function. We should also expect to see competitor platforms that use anything from a copyleft OSS license to proprietary licenses that support many of the same applications and data formats to operate just as we see now with Windows, Apple, and Linux-based OSs and competing content platforms such as ProQuest, EBSCO, Google, Amazon, and Apple.

SUMMARY

While there is an overlap with the type of libraries each ILS can serve, Evergreen, Koha, Invenio, and FOLIO have varying strengths and weaknesses that make them more suitable for some libraries than for others. Evergreen excels at serving library systems or consortia with many branches and diverse policies, including large metropolitan systems, school systems, and statewide systems, than it was originally designed for. Koha has demonstrated the most versatility in serving many different types of libraries, but small and medium public libraries are still the most popular types of libraries to adopt. Invenio, as its own OSS project, lacks all the development needed to compete with any modern ILS, but its architecture and what TIND has done with Invenio as a foundation to their proprietary ILS illustrates its promising potential. FOLIO is intended to be a direct competitor with proprietary LSPs such as Alma and WMS, and this explains its LSP architecture. Its sponsorship and large ARL oversight have caused it to take on a development path that might be described as a top-down approach compared to Koha's more organic growth.

However, FOLIO's partners are among the largest research/academic libraries in the world with the resources to put in proper development as well as companies like EBSCO and IndexData, which have a proven track record at getting successful products off the ground. This type of development hasn't really existed before in libraries. FOLIO, in the end, may be the least accessible for smaller libraries due to the resource-intensive nature of its design and the way it was developed. These characteristics may also make it feel less like an OSS project than other options, but time will tell. As a silver lining, this approach might allow for higher adoption rates of OSS as these characteristics might be viewed as less risky by library administration and, therefore, more appealing. As a library considers migrating their ILS, depending on a library's needs, all of these systems should be included in the review process. Hopefully, the details on each laid out in this chapter will serve as a useful guide on that journey.

NOTES

1. Marshall Breeding, "It's Time to Break the Mold of the Original ILS," *Computers in Libraries* (2007): 39–41.

2. Andrew Pace, "21st Century Libraries," *Journal of Library Administration* 49 (2009): 641–50.

3. Fadi P. Deek and James A. McHugh, *Open Source: Technology and Policy* (Cambridge and New York: Cambridge University Press, 2008), 4.

4. Thomas R. Kochtanek and Joseph R. Matthews, *Library Information Systems: from Library Automation to Distributed Information Access Solutions* (Westport, CT: Libraries Unlimited, 2002), 4.

5. "MARC Standards," *Library of Congress,* accessed March 7, 2020, http://www.loc.gov/marc/.

6. "What is ERP," *Oracle,* accessed March 7, 2020, https://www.oracle.com/applications/erp/what-is-erp.html.

7. Andrew Pace, "Dismantling Integrated Library Systems." *Library Journal* 129, no. 2 (February 1, 2004): 34–36.

8. Deek and McHugh, *Open Source: Technology and Policy.*

9. Pace, "Dismantling Integrated Library Systems."

10. "Libraries.org database," *Library Technology Guides*, accessed March 15, 2020, https://librarytechnology.org/libraries/search.pl?ILS=Koha&HQ=on.

11. Marshall Breeding, "Open Source Library Systems: The Current State of the Art," *Library Technology Reports* 53, no. 6 (August 2017): 11.

12. "Library management," *Catalyst*, accessed March 20, 2020, https://www.catalyst.net.nz/products/library-management-koha.

13. "History," *Koha-community.org*, accessed March 6, 2020, https://koha-community.org/about/history/.

14. Casey Bisson, "Open Source Software for Libraries," *Library Technology Reports* 43, no. 3 (May/June, 2007): 11.

15. "Project Organization," *Koha-community.org*, accessed March 5, 2020, https://koha-community.org/about/koha-project-organization/; "Horowhenua Library Trust Koha Committee Rules," *Koha-community.org*, accessed March 5, 2020, https://koha-community.org/about/koha-project-organization/horowhenua-library-trust-koha-committee-rules/.

16. "Zebra," *Indexdata.com*, accessed March 29, 2020, https://www.indexdata.com/resources/software/zebra/; Marshall Breeding, "Open Source Integrated Library Systems," *Library Technology Reports* 44, no. 8 (November/December 2008): 17.

17. "Koha adopts Elastic for Search functionality," *Library Technology Guides*, last modified February 12, 2020, accessed February 20, 2020, https://librarytechnology.org/pr/24921.

18. "History," *Koha-community.org*, accessed March 6, 2020, https://koha-community.org/about/history.

19. "Libraries.org database," *Library Technology Guides*, accessed March 7, 2020, https://librarytechnology.org/libraries/search.pl?ILS=Koha%20--%20BibLibre&HQ=on.

20. Breeding, "Open Source Library Systems."

21. "Libraries.org database," *Library Technology Guides*, accessed March 7, 2020, https://librarytechnology.org/libraries/search.pl?ILS=Koha%20--%20Bywater&HQ=on.

22. "Koha Expands in Australasia," *Catalyst*, February 12, 2020, accessed April 2, 2020, https://www.catalyst.net.nz/news/koha-expands-australasia.

23. "Libraries.org database," Library Technology Guides, accessed March 7, 2020, https://librarytechnology.org/libraries/search.pl?ILS=Koha%20--%20Catalyst&HQ=on ; Ibid., https://librarytechnology.org/libraries/search.pl?ILS=Koha%20--%20Calyx&HQ=on.

24. Breeding, "Open Source Library Systems."

25. "Libraries.org database," *Library Technology Guides*, accessed March 7, 2020, https://librarytechnology.org/libraries/search.pl?ILS=Koha%20--%20Equinox&HQ=on.

26. "Libraries.org database," *Library Technology Guides*, accessed April 23, 2020, https://librarytechnology.org/libraries/search.pl?ILS=Koha%20--%20Interleaf&HQ=on; "Interleaf Technology | Koha," *Interleaf*, accessed April 23, 2020, https://www.interleaf.ie/products-services/library-applications/koha/.

27. Breeding, "Open Source Integrated Library Systems," 22.

28. "Libraries.org database," *Library Technology Guides*, accessed March 7, 2020, https://librarytechnology.org/libraries/search.pl?ILS=Koha%20--%20PTFS&HQ=on.

29. "Koha Pakistan," *Koha Pakistan*, accessed March 23, 2020, https://kohapakistan.org/wp-content/uploads/2019/03/56041518_338716899977823_7558736200381397202_n.mp4.

30. *Library Technology Guides*, accessed March 7, 2020, https://librarytechnology.org/libraries/advanced/.

31. "About Us," *Evergreen*, accessed March 3, 2020, http://evergreen-ils.org/about-us.

32. "Libraries.org database," *Library Technology Guides*, accessed March 8, 2020, https://librarytechnology.org/libraries/search.pl?ILS=Evergreen&HQ=on.

33. "History," *King County Library System*, accessed March 20, 2020, https://kcls.org/history/.

34. Keith Ervin, "Patrons vexed by glitches in new library software," *Seattle Times*, January 30, 2011, accessed March 21, 2020, https://www.seattletimes.com/seattle-news/patrons-vexed-by-glitches-in-new-library-software/.

35. Matt Enis, "Developing Partnerships: As the Open Source ILS Movement Grows, Many Libraries are Outsourcing Technical Support and Development," *Library Journal* 138, no. 15 (September 15, 2013): 26.

36. Ervin, "Patrons Vexed."

37. Enis, "Developing Partnerships."

38. "Software Freedom Conservancy," *sfconservancy.org*, accessed March 23, 2020, https://sfconservancy.org.

39. "Software Freedom Conservancy," *Evergreen-Ils.org*, accessed March 23, 2020, https://evergreen-ils.org/conservancy.

40. "Evergreen Oversight Board Annual Meeting," *Evergreen DocuWiki*, accessed March 23, 2020, https://wiki.evergreen-ils.org/doku.php?id=governance:eob-minutes-2019-04-24.

41. "Libraries.org database," *Library Technology Guides*, accessed March 8, 2020, https://librarytechnology.org/libraries/search.pl?ILS=Evergreen -- Catalyst&HQ=on.

42. "Libraries.org database," *Library Technology Guides*, accessed March 8, 2020, https://librarytechnology.org/libraries/search.pl?ILS=Evergreen -- Equinox&HQ=on.

43. "Libraries.org database," *Library Technology Guides*, accessed March 8, 2020, https://librarytechnology.org/libraries/search.pl?ILS=Evergreen -- Emerald&HQ=on.

44. "Libraries.org database," *Library Technology Guides*, accessed March 8, 2020, https://librarytechnology.org/libraries/search.pl?ILS=Evergreen -- MOBIUS&HQ=on.

45. "About Invenio: A Brief Story of an Open Source Project," *Invenio-software.org*, accessed March 15, 2020, https://invenio-software.org/about.

46. "The Birth of the Web," *CERN*, accessed March 15, 2020, https://home.cern/science/computing/birth-web.

47. "About Invenio," *Invenio-software.org*.

48. "License," *Github.com*, accessed February 28, 2020, https://github.com/inveniosoftware/invenio-app-ils/blob/master/LICENSE.

49. "TIND ILS," *Tind*, accessed February 29, 2020, https://info.tind.io/ILS.

50. "Governance," *Inveniosoftware.org*, accessed February 29, 2020, https://inveniosoftware.org/governance.

51. C. Sean Burns, "Academic Libraries and Automation: A Historical Reflection on Ralph Halsted Parker," *Portal: Library and the Academy*, 14, 1, (2014), 87–102; Simon Barron and Andrew Preater, "Critical Systems Librarianship," In: *The Politics of Theory and the Practice of Critical Librarianship*, (Sacramento, CA: Library Juice Press, 2018) 87–113.

52. Todd Carpenter, "Open Library Environment (OLE) Project – Planning open ILS systems," NISO, August 2008, accessed March 30, 2020, https://www.niso.org/niso-io/2008/08/open-library-environment-ole-project-planning-open-ils-systems; The Andrew W. Mellon Foundation, accessed March 30, 2020, https://mellon.org/; Breeding, "Open Source Library Systems," 25.

53. Carpenter, "Open Library Environment (OLE) Project."

54. "OLE," Open Library Environment, accessed March 30, 2020, https://openlibraryenvironment.org/.

55. Marshall Breeding, "Perceptions 2018: An International Survey of Library Automation," *Library Technology Guides*, accessed April 10, 2020, https://librarytechnology.org/perceptions/2018/#worldshare.

56. "Libraries.org database," *Library Technology Guides*, accessed April 10, 2020, https://librarytechnology.org/libraries/search.pl?ILS=Worldshare Management Services&HQ=on.

57. *IndexData*, accessed March 29, 2020, https://www.indexdata.com.

58. "YAZ," *Index Data*, accessed March 29, 2020, https://www.indexdata.com/resources/software/yaz; "Zebra," *IndexData*, accessed March 29, 2020, https://www.indexdata.com/resources/software/zebra.

59. "FOLIO Platform Visualization," *folio.org*, accessed April 8, 2020, https://www.folio.org/wp-content/uploads/2018/08/PDF-2016_08_FOLIO-Platform-Visualization.pdf.

60. Josh Evan, "Mastering Chaos - A Netflix Guide to Microservices," *InfoQ*, accessed April 9, 2020, https://www.youtube.com/watch?v=CZ3wIuvmHeM.

61. "Explain DB schema and performance issues," *folio.org*, accessed April 10, 2020, https://dev.folio.org/faqs/explain-database-schema.

62. "Definition of the Okapi-Stripes Platform, FOLIO LSP Base and FOLIO LSP Extended Apps," *wiki.folio.org*, accessed April 10, 2020, https://wiki.folio.org/display/TC/Definition+of+the+Okapi-Stripes+Platform%2C+FOLIO+LSP+Base+and+FOLIO+LSP+Extended+Apps.

63. Barron and Preater, "Critical Systems Librarianship."

64. "Libraries.org database," *Library Technology Guides*, accessed November 12, 2020, https://librarytechnology.org/libraries/search.pl?ILS=FOLIO&HQ=on.

65. Keven Liu, "FOLIO in China," *WOLFcon2020*, accessed April 8, 2020, https://www.youtube.com/watch?v=p-_llucfXkY.

66. Breeding, "Perceptions 2018," https://librarytechnology.org/perceptions/2018/#bywater.

67. Matt Enis, "Open Source FOLIO LSP Nears Launch, as Lehigh U. Library Partners with Index Data," *Library Journal*, November 7, 2019, accessed April 8, 2020, https://www.libraryjournal.com/?detailStory=open-source-folio-lsp-nears-launch-as-lehigh-partners-index-data.

68. "Introducing FOLIO — A new collaboration bringing libraries, service providers and developers together to speed innovation and redefine the future of library automation," *folio.org*, June 24, 2016, accessed April 8, 2020, https://www.folio.org/about/news-events/article/introducing-folio-a-new-collaboration-bringing-libraries-service-providers-and-developers-together-to-speed-innovation-and-redefine-the-future-of-library-automation.

4

Open Source and Digital Repositories

When compared to integrated library systems, digital repositories are a relative newcomer to the library technology ecosystem. A digital repository is a catch-all term for software solutions that may be used by cultural heritage institutions to store, document, preserve, manage, or provide, either internal or external to the institution, access to—or any combination of these functions—multimedia content. Digital repositories serve multiple purposes within cultural heritage institutions. Depending on the digital repository software, organizations may use these tools to provide access to or preserve born-digital or digitized content. Additionally, these platforms may be used to preserve and provide access to content for historical, educational, administrative, routine operation, or research purposes. Most of these platforms fulfill a variety of these functions, but each software has its relative strengths and weaknesses depending on its intended use. The unique characteristics of each of these software platforms are determined by their history, the technology upon which they are built, and the social ecosystem that supports them.

At the outset, it is necessary to clarify the meaning of terms that are often used in association with the software platforms we will discuss throughout this chapter. A digital asset management system (DAMS) "is an integrated suite of infrastructure components used to capture, catalog, store, and manage digital assets and to expose those assets to creative tools for producing video, audio, Web, and print content."[1] Digital asset management has become an increasingly important component to ensure the preservation and continued access to digital content. Cultural heritage institutions are not the only users of DAMS. DAMS has value for almost any organization that creates digital content and ensures its access well into the future.

An institutional repository (IR) is similar in many ways to DAMS. In fact, some of the open source solutions we discuss in the chapter have both DAMS and IR applications. DSpace is a perfect example of this phenomenon. What primarily distinguishes these two systems is not so much the technologies that underpin them. Rather, the key distinction is the ends these systems serve. Clifford Lynch has defined university-based institutional repositories as "a set of services that a university offers to the members of its community for the management and dissemination of digital materials created by the institution and its community members."[2] IRs represent a subset of digital repositories and have become an important tool used by institutions—universities, in particular—to capture their intellectual output. IR content may consist of pre-print publications created by the institution's researchers, an organization's policies and reports, digital copies of conference presentations, student research, electronic theses and dissertations, and various other content. IRs have also been used to house and display digitized content of historical significance to an institution.

Digital collection software rounds out the three major terms used to describe the systems that follow in this chapter. Digital collection software is primarily focused on public access to digital materials. Omeka is a specific example of this type of digital repository. Omeka is described on its own site as "a leading open source web publishing platform for digital collections."[3] Digital collection software such as Omeka can contain add-ons for digital exhibits, for example, to enhance the accessibility of digital content.

While the terms outlined above are by no means the only ones used in reference to digital repositories, they do serve to demonstrate the varied nature of digital repositories and highlight why digital repositories can be a minefield for people who are new to exploring these forms of software. For any librarian, curator, or archivist considering either implementing a new digital repository or migrating to a new one, recognizing these terms can help one to determine the primary purposes these different platforms were created to serve.

HISTORY AND CURRENT STATE

The usage of the terms institutional repository, digital asset management system, and digital collection software not only imply distinct purposes. They also imply a distinct history in the development of digital repositories.

Digital Asset Management Systems

Digital Asset Management Systems (DAMS) as information technology tools historically preceded IRs, even though they share many similarities with IRs within cultural heritage institutions. The first DAMS were developed by large companies like IBM and Content Management Systems in the early 1990s to assist large commercial companies in internally managing their digital content.[4] Even though proprietary DAMS were developed in the early 1990s for museums, it would not be until the early 2000s that DAMS solutions would be developed with libraries, archives, and museums in mind. Perhaps the most well-known DAMS from this period still known and in use among smaller libraries, museums, and archives is CONTENTdm by OCLC.[5] Some of the OSS platforms developed in the first decade of the twentieth century—among which are Fedora, DSpace, and Islandora—are commonly referred to as both IRs and DAMS.[6]

Institutional Repositories

The conceptual groundwork for what would eventually become known as the IR was laid in the final decade of the twentieth century. Envisioned as an alternative method of disseminating esoteric scholarly research where there was little to no market, the institutional repository was conceptualized to increase the speed with which scholars could share their research and decrease the cost accrued to traditional customers of esoteric scholarly publishing.[7]

From their inception, the first institutional repository platforms were open source. Eprints, the first institutional repository developed, was released to the public in 2001, with the source code openly available to any who had an interest.[8] Eprints was quickly followed by the release of DSpace in 2002, a collaborative effort between developers at MIT and HP Labs.[9] Building upon the Fedora software after its public release in 2003, Islandora was developed in 2006 by the University of Prince Edward Island's library.[10] Hydra, what is now known as Samvera, began in 2008 and—like Islandora—was developed on top of the Fedora platform.[11] Omeka, funded by the Institute of Museum and Library Services (IMLS), was developed by the Roy Rosenzweig Center for History and New Media to be a simple platform for small libraries, archives, and museums to share their digital collections on the web. It was first launched in 2008.[12] All of these software products, along with their respective communities, have developed and grown in recent years. When it comes to institutional repositories, cultural heritage institutions have several OSS products to pick from, with a variety of options now available for hosting and support. Knowing which product best meets one's needs requires careful consideration of the various technical capabilities of the platform, the health of the community supporting it, and the assistance an institution might expect to receive with whichever solution it chooses.

OPEN SOURCE OPTIONS

DSpace

> Community: https://duraspace.org/dspace/community/
> Code: https://github.com/DSpace/DSpace
> Live Demo: https://github.com/DSpace/DSpace

DSpace is not only technically one of the oldest open source digital repository solutions under consideration, but it is also by far the most popular institutional repository solution available. A filtered search of OpenDOAR, an open-access directory for discovering digital repositories, with results limited to "DSpace," returns a result of over 2,000 entries representing institutional, governmental, and other types of organizations worldwide.[13] As mentioned previously, DSpace was the result of collaboration between MIT Libraries

DSpace

How would you describe the DSpace community?
A great international community that is very active on both the user and development side, with many user groups and events going on in various parts of the world.

How has DSpace benefitted your organization?
Today, we could say that we were lucky when we chose DSpace as our "main IR solution" more than fifteen years ago. From the beginning, DSpace (as an open source solution) has been open in all aspects. DSpace is part of an open source community, and its software is based on open standards and protocols. By using DSpace, we have been able to embrace the open access movement. DSpace has also helped our institution to share our academic production and helped us to be more visible to the world.

Jordan Piščanc
University of Trieste
Trieste, Italy

and Hewlett-Packard. The primary concern of the developers of DSpace was to ensure the long-term preservation of digital content created by various departments, schools, and labs across MIT.[14]

Background and Current State

DSpace is an application written primarily using the Java programming language and uses a browser-based interface for day-to-day administration, submission, and access. DSpace is licensed under the permissive BSD license, a point that will become important later in this section. While DSpace requires other software to function (e.g., Apache Maven, Apache Ant, PostgreSQL, and Tomcat), all of these applications are also open source and freely available through traditional installation methods on Windows, OSX, and Linux. DSpace stores data in a—either PostgreSQL or Oracle—relational database and uses Apache Solr, an open source indexing software, to provide browse and search functionality. DSpace supports the usage of Qualified Dublin Core metadata and is capable of translating this metadata upon import and export into both MaRC or MODS metadata formats. Additionally, DSpace supports the harvesting of its metadata using the standard OAI-PMH protocol, an important protocol for ensuring interoperability with other library systems. DSpace is capable of storing all content types, including file types for documents, images, video, audio, and datasets.[15]

While DSpace has its own built-in authentication for managing users, it can also integrate with an institution's preexisting authentication mechanisms such as LDAP and Shibboleth.[16] Another strength of DSpace is the granularity of its permissions. Restriction to content can range from the whole site all the way down to the item level. For institutions that need the level of protection for their assets, the selection of DSpace may play a significant factor. DSpace also provides a quick and simple solution for backing up and restoring content using AIP backup files. Again, a DSpace administrator can either back up an entire site or even a single item using this method, and the administrator can use these files to perform restoration actions if necessary.[17] Finally, DSpace can also incorporate extensions from third-party vendors to extend DSpace's functionality. Extensions may serve to improve the end user's experience, or they may improve the consistency of metadata. Because DSpace is licensed under a permissive license—the BSD license—vendors are capable of developing and selling these extensions. Digital repositories licensed under more restrictive license types—like GPL licenses—may prevent this sort of activity. None of the preceding statements should be construed as a negative aspect of the DSpace community. However, a library, archive, or museum should at least be aware that these extensions may come with a price tag and not be readily available free of cost. A full list of publicly available add-ons can be found on the DSpace wiki.[18]

DSpace is currently on major release 6.0, but version 7.0 is already in the beta phase of development. Significant development effort has been put into DSpace 7.0 in order to update the user interface to meet the standards of modern front-end development and design to improve the end-user experience.

Community and Service Providers

Libraries, archives, and museums that wish to implement an open source repository such as DSpace but lack personnel or funding to manage the repository internally have several options with providers located around the globe.

LYRASIS (https://www.lyrasis.org/Pages/Main.aspx): Following a merger with DuraSpace in 2019, LYRASIS now offers a hosted, turnkey digital repository solution using DSpace called DSpaceDirect.[19] Based out of Atlanta, Georgia, LYRASIS offers hosting solutions for a variety of other library, archive, and museum software. DSpaceDirect is a fully-hosted solution and includes server configuration, backup, and upgrade at no extra cost. Pricing for customer support is broken up into tiers, with ten service support requests available for free annually by default. Other plans with more support are available. Additional add-on packages, including extended support access—for an additional cost—are available. Examples of extended support include custom URL configuration, IP-based restricted access, and migration assistance from a locally hosted instance of DSpace to DSpaceDirect.[20]

4Science (https://www.4science.it/en/): Based in Italy, 4Science is a certified DSpace partner and has been a service provider for DSpace since 2015. With two full-time developers who contribute to the DSpace codebase and as a representative member of the DSpace Steering Committee, 4Science has a vested interest in the success and development of DSpace.[21] 4Science offers services to assist in the installation and configuration of DSpace, either in an institution's self-hosted environment or in a 4Science-controlled environment. 4Science also sells maintenance and support packages with varying levels of service level agreements (SLAs). Customized software solutions as well as pre-developed add-ons to extend the functionality of DSpace are available through 4Science's services. Finally, 4Science also sells training and consultation services. 4Science represents a perfect example of a service provider with a highly customizable solution for open source implementation.[22]

Atmire (https://www.atmire.com): Atmire, like 4Science, is a certified DSpace partner and registered service provider. Based in Belgium and the United States, Atmire offers a full-service SaaS implementation of DSpace, called DSpace Express. This implementation includes custom branding for your institution, routine upgrades to DSpace, Single Sign-On (SSO) integration, data backups, and support through a DSpace Express subscription. DSpace Express is hosted by Atmire in Amazon's cloud service, Amazon Web Services (AWS).[23] DSpace Express is an ideal solution for institutions that wish to get up and running with a digital repository quickly and whose custom needs are minimal. Atmire also provides customized DSpace implementations. Custom DSpace services include needs assessment and assistance in migrating, upgrading, or implementing DSpace integrations. Additionally, Atmire sells add-ons to enhance DSpace functionality and can even develop customized solutions to meet an institution's particular needs. Institutions may also purchase support services for an on-premises deployment of DSpace or an Atmire cloud-hosted deployment over which the institution would be able to control code or configuration changes to DSpace.[24]

The Library Code GmbH (https://www.the-library-code.de/): The Library Code represents the last of DSpace's certified service providers. Headquartered in Germany and founded by Pascal-Nicolas Becker—a member of the DSpace Committer Group—the Library Code offers pre-implementation consultation, assistance with DSpace installation, custom add-on development, hosting, and training services. Hosting is available using the Library Code's servers or in a data environment of the institution's choosing.[25]

Future Outlook

It has been over seventeen years since DSpace was first released to the public. During the period since, DSpace has seen six major releases, with the newest major release in progress. Furthermore, it has become the most popular software for institutional repositories. With fourteen developers actively contributing to its codebase and numerous service providers located all over the globe, it is hard to imagine a future where DSpace doesn't play a crucial role in supporting cultural heritage institutions as they seek to preserve and provide access to its digital content.

EPrints

> Community: https://www.eprints.org/uk/index.php/category/community/#
> Code: https://github.com/eprints/eprints3.4
> Live Demo: http://demo.eprints-hosting.org/

EPrints is the oldest digital repository considered in this chapter. The idea for what would become EPrints originated when Stevan Harnad and Les Carr promised a simple turnkey repository at the initial OAI meeting held in Santa

Fe, New Mexico, in 1999.[26] EPrints was originally developed by researchers at the University of Southampton School of Electronics and Computer Science for the CogPrints archive, a disciplinary electronic archive for storing self-archived pre-print publications in the area of cognitive science.[27] The source code for the CogPrints platform would later be released under the GPL open source license.[28] On July 1, 2002, the EPrints project would officially join the GNU project.[29] Today, there are over 600 entities listed in OpenDOAR with EPrints as their digital repository.[30] The EPrints GitHub repository for version 3.4, EPrints's most current version, lists eight different contributors to the EPrints codebase with updates to the master branch being committed weekly.

Background and Current State

EPrints uses a LAMP stack architecture and is written primarily in the Perl programming language. By default, EPrints supports the storage of descriptive metadata using the simple Dublin Core metadata standard. The software can, however, export metadata in common formats such as MODS and METS. EPrints complies with OAI-PMH for metadata extraction and supports the SWORD protocol for ingesting digital objects and their associated metadata. EPrints does not support backup through the use of AIP files.[31] EPrints administrators, if an institution is considering implementing this solution, will need to use traditional backup methods using Linux and relational database administration tools. While EPrints can store and manage files in pretty much any format, the software has not been optimized to work with datasets and may require customization to get EPrints to meet an institution's needs. Additionally, bulk import of new materials does not work out of the box and requires enhancement.

Community and Service Providers

The open source community supporting EPrints provides several avenues of communication. Perhaps the best place to start learning more about EPrints would be its wiki.[32] The wiki contains background information on EPrints, instructions on installing and configuring Eprints, tutorials for using EPrints, and contact information for further questions.[33] The EPrints community also manages a mailing list for those who wish to ask technical questions related to EPrints. There are even user groups in the United Kingdom and Germany for any institutions in this region that are interested in getting involved with the EPrints community.[34]

EPrints Services (https://www.eprints.org/us/services/): EPrints Services, based out of Southampton in the United Kingdom, is the only known service provider for the EPrints repository platform. EPrints Services exists "to promote the use of repositories and to provide a sustainable funding stream to guarantee the future development and support of EPrints Open Source software."[35]

EPrints Services provides consulting, training, hosting, and support services with a variety of options for institutions to meet their needs.[36] For institutions in the United States, EPrints Services has a history of supporting EPrints institutions in the United States, including institutions such as the California Institute of Technology, NOAA, and the Fred Hutchinson Cancer Research Center.[37]

Future Outlook

As the oldest digital repository for libraries, archives, and museums, EPrints has seen slow but steady development over its lifetime. With version 3.4's release in the middle of 2016, it had been almost five years between minor releases (i.e., 3.3 to 3.4). In comparison, the timespan between 3.3 and 3.2 of EPrints was approximately eighteen months. While this observation by no means is an objective indicator of a slowing in the development of EPrints—it may, for example, indicate ambitious improvements to the codebase—it is still a significant gap in releases.[38] Nevertheless, during this same time period of slower development, EPrints implementations among institutions have grown significantly from 500 implementations in 2013 to over 600 implementations today, a growth of over 15 percent.[39] While the influence of EPrints appears to be felt primarily in the United Kingdom and Europe, there is plenty of room for growth internationally.

Islandora

> Community: https://groups.google.com/forum/#!forum/islandora
> Code: https://github.com/Islandora/islandora
> Live Demo: https://future.islandora.ca/

Like many of the open source systems discussed in this guide, Islandora originated when a specific library sought to develop a solution to meet its specific use cases. Developed by the library at the University of Prince Edward Island (UPEI) in Canada, Islandora was built to provide a front-end to interface with the Fedora repository software. Fedora, a back-end repository solution for storing, managing, and preserving digital content, is just one piece of a more user-friendly digital repository solution. Thus, Islandora was born. When Islandora was first developed, the UPEI was using Moodle, Drupal, and

OJS as front-end solutions with Fedora. Eventually, the developers at UPEI decided to focus on developing the Drupal-based front-end as a framework for a digital repository platform.[40] In less than fifteen years of development, Islandora has expanded from its original environment at UPEI to over 300 institutions across the globe.[41]

Background and Current State

Islandora, or what is also referred to as the Islandora stack, consists of numerous components, the most significant of which are a Drupal front-end as a user-friendly interface, a Fedora repository for back-end digital object management, and Solr for index and search functionality.[42] Islandora itself is really a Drupal module created to tailor the web interface to function as a digital repository.[43] Drupal is used in a variety of other contexts, apart from digital repository solutions, as a framework for quickly building websites—Drupal is essentially an open source—GPL licensed—content management software (CMS).[44] Combined with additional components to facilitate efficient communications between Islandora and Fedora, the Islandora stack makes for a complete digital repository solution.

Because Islandora was created to extend the functionality of the Fedora repository software and not retread the ground of the Fedora community, the Islandora and the Fedora software communities have mutually benefited. The result is a partnership where the Islandora software can excel at creating a user-friendly experience for information professionals while the Fedora community develops its repository to ensure a high-quality management platform that ensures access and integrity to digital objects in the long term.

By default, Islandora supports the storage and maintenance of all file types, although the user experience among different file types will vary. Islandora, since it is built on Drupal, supports an easily customizable and efficient user interface. Examples of out-of-the-box functionality include authority linking, media conversion, custom-hidden fields and permission control, bulk import using CSV files, and bulk metadata modification customizable collection views.

The functionality of Islandora can easily be extended to support OAI-PMH harvesting, OCR processing, and usage statistics. Islandora also supports linked data functionality, a further testimony as an up-to-date and powerful solution for libraries that wish to take advantage of the most current in metadata standards.[45]

Community and Service Providers

For some institutions, an overview of the details in the previous sections or a glimpse at Islandora's technical documentation may be overwhelming. For those without the in-house expertise to configure a private cloud or a locally hosted on-site installation of Islandora, there are several service providers available with years of experience hosting and supporting Islandora that can help even small institutions to implement this digital repository.

discoverygarden (https://www.discoverygarden.ca/): Headquartered in Charlottetown, Prince Edward Island, Canada—the birthplace of the Islandora project—discoverygarden, Inc. has been supporting institutions since 2010 in implementing Islandora instances. For institutions looking to get started quickly with Islandora as their first digital repository, discoverygarden offers a SaaS implementation of Islandora. This option can be great for institutions that require little in the way of customizations. Discoverygarden's services are customizable to meet an institution's needs and include options for installation, migration, monitoring, branding customization, hosting, and support.[46]

LYRASIS (https://www.lyrasis.org/Pages/Main.aspx): LYRASIS has become one of the leading services providers of OSS for cultural heritage institutions over the past decade. LYRASIS offers hosting solutions, including Islandora, DSpace, ArchivesSpace, Library Simplified, and CollectionSpace. Islandora hosting includes a variety of support packages depending on an institution's perceived needs.

Born-Digital (https://born-digital.com/): Located in Hadley, Massachusetts, Born-Digital specializes in Islandora hosting and operates by developing a custom-tailored plan for implementing Islandora that is based on institutional specifications. Born-Digital uses a transparent multi-phase plan that is broken up into an initial phase of assessing need and outlining work to be done, a second phase in which the installation is built to specification and data—if it already exists—is ingested into the new installation, and a final phase where Born-Digital provides maintenance and support for your Islandora instance. Born-Digital's process for implementing Islandora is simple and clear. Additional services such as consultation and customization are also available.[47] Born-Digital method of assisting institutions in implementing Islandora demonstrates the benefit of working with a service provider that specializes in a particular software.

Digital Echidna (https://echidna.ca/): Based out of London, Ontario, Digital Echidna is unique among Islandora service providers in that it is a company that specializes in Drupal development.[48] Islandora, as a Drupal module, is just one of the many Drupal customization services they provide. For more information on Digital Echidna's quality of service, there are over forty reviews at https://clutch.com/profile/digital-echidna that testify to the quality of their work.

Agile Humanities Agency (https://agilehumanities.ca/): Based out of Toronto, Agile Humanities Agency has a decade of experience working with Islandora. The developers at Agile Humanities actively contribute to the development of the Islandora codebase. In addition to contributing to the development of Islandora, Agile Humanities also provides hosting and support services.

Future Outlook

Over the past fourteen years, Islandora has demonstrated itself to be a viable solution for institutions of all sizes. With the advent of hosting services and the expertise service providers afford libraries, OSS, like Islandora, is within reach of even the smallest institutions. Islandora has gained steam throughout its lifetime and is surrounded by active development and user-group communities. Institutions that plan to either self-host Islandora or contract out hosting will be entrusting the future of their digital repository to one of the most active open source communities in libraries, archives, and museums.

Samvera/Hyrax

> Community: https://groups.google.com/forum/#!forum/samvera-community/join
> Code: https://github.com/samvera
> Live Demo: http://repo.samvera.org/

With the ultimate success in the development of the Fedora repository software, and because of the specific function Fedora fulfills as a data management platform, it fell on individual institutions to develop front-end interfaces for working with Fedora on a daily basis. We've already seen one example of this phenomenon in what would become Islandora out of the University of Prince Edward Island. The Samvera project is another example of a

Samvera

> *Can you share the story of Samvera at your organization?*
> Our two consortia, The Pennsylvania Academic Library Consortium, Inc. (PALCI), and Private Academic Library Network of Indiana (PALNI), represent ninety-four academic libraries in Indiana,

Pennsylvania, New Jersey, West Virginia, and New York. Many of our libraries are seeking affordable options for institutional repositories or other digital asset management services and aren't finding them in the commercial market. In addition, participation in the open source community is out of reach for many due to a lack of adequate staffing and easy-to-implement solutions. PALCI and PALNI have been working together since 2017 to develop and pilot a shared repository service using Hyku, Samvera's multi-tenant repository solution, through shared grant funding. As we develop the software to fit our shared needs, we are also developing a low-cost, sustainable business model for the future that sees out two consortia working together to create a flexible, scalable service for our library communities.

How would you describe the Samvera community?
The Samvera community is highly organized and collaborative. The institutions participating in the software development are committed to working together and building community-based solutions to digital resource management and access. We believe our consortia represent a new perspective in the community, as we represent many libraries, both small and large, that would otherwise not be able to be involved. In the time we have been involved in Samvera, we have seen an increase in outreach and documentation that welcomes newcomers and those with less technology experience.

How has Samvera benefitted your organization?
When we were looking at viable solutions for our repository goals, Hyku was the one that fit the bill best: open source, multi-tenant, and easy to deploy. However, it lacked some key configuration options and features to allow us to effectively deliver services across consortia. Through generous IMLS grant funding, we have been able to build out Hyku to meet our needs in ways that would not have been possible with other options. This has allowed us to expand the capacity for repository services at our member institutions and offered institutions the opportunity to participate in an international community, shaping the direction of future library services.

Gretchen Gueguen
Partnership for Academic Library Collaboration & Innovation (PALCI)
Drexel Hill, Pennsylvania, USA

community—in this case, at least, it included initially the University of Virginia, the University of Hull, Stanford University, and Fedora Commons—developing a user-friendly interface for working with Fedora. Stakeholders from these institutions recognized that it would be more beneficial to work together to develop a front-end solution for working with Fedora that was modular enough to cater to the specific needs of each institution without requiring individual institutions to configure unnecessary components for local use.[49] The three educational institutions mentioned above agreed to use the web application framework Ruby on Rails to create the modular front-end they had in mind. By the end of 2011, the partners had delivered a working version of what they would call Hydra available for use.[50] The name Hydra evokes the multi-headed mythological creature from ancient Greek myth. Fedora is the body of the Hydra project, and the various use cases represent the heads. Individual institutions had the ability to make use of whatever heads were necessary to meet local needs for working with Fedora. In less than a year, the Hydra project had grown from the original three institutions to ten. Today, the Hydra project enjoys over thirty partner institutions and numerous other implementers involved in the support and use of Samvera.[51]

Background and Current State

To date, the Samvera community has almost sixty institutions that have implemented some variation of Samvera solutions, with other institutions in the process of implementing.[52] While not exclusively so, many of the institutions actively involved in the Samvera community are larger research universities. Development of Samvera over the past two years has been focused on developing out-of-the-box repository solutions such as Hyku to lower the barrier many smaller institutions might encounter in attempting to use Samvera's framework.

Community and Service Providers

CoSector, University of London (http://cosector.com/research-technologies): Based out of London in the United Kingdom, CoSector has been working with open source software since 2007.[53] While CoSector also provides hosting and support for services like Eprints, Open Journal Systems, and Haplo Repositories, they have been hosting, supporting, and developing solutions with Samvera since 2017.[54]

Cottage Labs (https://cottagelabs.com/): Cottage Labs, a UK-based service provider, actively contributes to the Samvera community and provides customized development solutions for Samvera. Cottage Labs is currently working to offer a SaaS implementation of Samvera, referred to as "Willow."

Data Curation Experts (https://curationexperts.com/): Data Curation Experts is headquartered in Minneapolis, Minnesota, and their services are focused primarily on the Samvera platform. Data Curation Experts provides assistance in repository planning and design, custom software development for Samvera functionality, managing and hosting Samvera instances, and training, among other customizable services.[55] Among other interesting features of working with Data Curation Experts is their discounting structure with benefits for clients who are willing to make contracted code open source.[56]

Notch8 (https://www.notch8.com/): Located in San Diego, California, Notch8 is a software development company that specializes in Ruby and Ruby on Rails development. Among its noted collaborators for developing custom Samvera solutions are Yale University, UCLA, Rutgers University, and UC San Diego, among others. In addition to offering custom solutions to Samvera implementation, Notch8 also has its own SaaS solution for Samvera called HykuUP.[57]

Ubiquity (https://ubiquitypress.com): While Ubiquity Press may be known primarily as a publisher, it's also a Samvera partner and host for Samvera instances. Ubiquity's hosting service, referred to as Ubiquity Repositories, is a great solution for both small and large libraries. Ubiquity has experience creating multi-tenant repositories and has experience migrating libraries from proprietary systems and boasts no vendor lock-in.[58]

Future Outlook

Samvera consists of a small yet dedicated group of partners to oversee its implementation. While Samvera has maintained between thirty and forty partners consistently over the past few years, the Samvera community has been serious about building community buy-in. Because many of the institutions supporting Samvera consist of large research universities and other institutions with funding to back the community, Samvera has been able to sustain development, build interest, and create an innovative repository solution that is flexible enough to meet the needs of even the largest institutions. Interest and involvement in the Samvera community have grown over the years, and as the Samvera developers continue to develop out-of-the-box solutions like Hyku, that interest is only going to continue to grow, as the barriers to entry for small-to-mid-sized institutions dissipate.

Omeka

Community: https://omeka.org/category/community/
Code: https://github.com/omeka/Omeka (Omeka Classic); https://github.com/omeka/omeka-s (Omeka S)
Live Demo: http://dev.omeka.org/omeka-s-sandbox/login[59]

Omeka, a Swahili term meaning "to display," is a fitting name for this software. Omeka is an easy-to-implement, user-friendly digital collection software that focuses primarily on the display and access of digital content. The idea for Omeka was developed by the Roy Rosenzweig Center for History and New Media (RRCHNM) and funded by the Institute of Museum and Library Services (IMLS) from 2007–2010. The Omeka community recognized that many cultural heritage institutions in the first decade of the millennium, both great and small, either lacked a web presence entirely or published digital content that often didn't follow standards to make their content accessible on the web. Omeka was created to solve this issue by developing a usable platform that could be extended with plugins and APIs. From their desire to create a truly simple web publishing platform that was 508 compliant, met common metadata standards for digital objects in cultural heritage institutions, and exposed their collection to search engines, the Omeka community—led by RRCHNM—developed a digital collection solution that is used by thousands of institutions and individuals who wish to expose and share their collections over the Internet.

Background and Current State

Since it was first released in 2008, Omeka has continued to grow in popularity among small cultural heritage institutions. RRCHNM's solution for hosting sites, called Omeka.net, alone has over 30,000 sites. While there have been many developments in Omeka since its initial release, especially with the developments of additional plugins to extend the functionality of Omeka, one of the most significant projects has been the development of what is known as Omeka S. Omeka S is a form of Omeka that provides a central administration interface for multiple Omeka sites. Other additions to Omeka S functionality include exposing metadata in Omeka to the Linked Open Data environment. Omeka S also harnesses Resource Description Framework tools to meet Semantic Web standards. Omeka S was developed to meet the needs and concerns of larger cultural heritage institutions, although they would by no means be the only ones to benefit from the Omeka S platform. Both Omeka S and Omeka, what is also often referred to as Omeka Classic, are built primarily in PHP and use a LAMP stack architecture for deploying their solutions on the web. There are one hundred registered plugins for the Omeka Classic platform, and many of the most popular plugins are available with the Omeka.net hosted solution. Plugins that extend the functionality of Omeka include bulk import of metadata via CSV files, batch item upload, exhibit building, reporting tools, OCR of PDFs, extended Dublin Core, and many other plugins. Installation of plugins and administration of Omeka sites are simple, and development has focused on making Omeka user-friendly to the user without systems administration expertise.

Community and Service Providers

Omeka.net (https://www.omeka.net/): Omeka.net is RRCHNM's site for hosting instances of Omeka Classic and is Omeka's primary SaaS platform. Omeka.net has hosting plans that range from $35 per year to $1,000 per year. Subscription plans vary based on price, storage allotted, the number of sites possible per account, plugins, and themes available. If needed, the Omeka development team also offers planning, custom theming and design, extension development, and a support plan as services.

While there don't appear to be hosting options for Omeka Classic and Omeka S like the other digital repositories considered in this chapter, the Omeka manual does list several infrastructure providers that could easily accommodate Omeka installations.

Future Outlook

Over the past twelve years, the Omeka community, and its software, has established itself as a mainstay within the library, archive, and museum ecosystem. With tens of thousands of installations, and even more users of Omeka, the future potential of Omeka only continues to grow. With the development of Omeka S, the Omeka community has sought to broaden its potential user base by creating functionality often prized by larger cultural heritage institutions. Development of Omeka and Omeka S shows no signs of slowing. For the near future, at least, Omeka isn't going anywhere.

Since the turn of the millennium, digital repositories have established themselves as integral components of the library technology ecosystem. From the earliest days of EPrints, DSpace, and Fedora, to the current context where additions like Islandora, Samvera, and Omeka have each built their own communities to meet specific institutional needs, digital repositories are becoming increasingly important in helping libraries fulfill their responsibilities to their institutions and their communities. All of these open source communities have strong communities of developers, users, and other stakeholders that have only continued to grow over the years. Sponsorship and funding from LYRASIS, the Andrew W. Mellon Foundation, and the Institute of Museum and Library Services have only strengthened these communities over the years, and service providers to assist libraries with hosting, support, and development are added to their respective communities each year. Gone are the days when libraries needed in-house expertise with on-site infrastructure. Open source options for digital repositories, with the rise of cloud computing, have never been easier to implement for libraries both large and small. As each solution discussed in this chapter has its own unique strengths and weaknesses—with none of them being a perfect solution for every library out there—libraries must carefully weigh what digital repository solution works best for them.

NOTES

1. Alan McCord, "Overview of Digital Asset Management Systems," EDUCAUSE Evolving Technologies Committee, September 6, 2002, retrieved from https://www.researchgate.net/publication/200026908_Overview_of_Digital_Asset_Management_Systems.

2. Clifford A. Lynch, "Institutional Repositories: Essential Infrastructure for Scholarship in the Digital Age," *portal: Libraries and the Academy* 3, no. 2 (2003): 327.

3. "Project," Roy Rosenzweig Center for History and New Media, accessed July 25, 2020, https://omeka.org/about/project/.

4. Richard W. Boss, "Digital Asset Management Systems," *PLA TechNotes*, October 28, 2009, https://alair.ala.org/bitstream/handle/11213/258/Digital%20Asset%20Management%20 Systems.pdf?sequence=80&isAllowed=y.

5. "CONTENTdm," OCLC.org, accessed August 4, 2020, https://www.oclc.org/en/contentdm.html.

6. While FEDORA, which is an acronym for Flexible Extensible Digital Object Repository, is an incredibly important development in the history of digital repositories within the cultural heritage institution ecosystem, it is not considered among our list of digital repositories. Since FEDORA is not a stand-alone solution for most organizations in our target audience, it will only be mentioned in relation to other projects that use FEDORA as a part of their digital repository architecture.

7. James Joseph O'Donnell and Ann Okerson, *Scholarly Journals at the Crossroads: A Subversive Proposal for Electronic Publishing* (Washington, DC: Office of Scientific & Academic Publishing, Association of Research Libraries, 1995), 17. Retrieved from https://catalog.hathitrust.org/Record/003013520.

8. Robert Tansley and Steven Harnad, "Eprints.org Software for Creating Institutional and Individual Open Access," *D-Lib Magazine* (October 2000). Retrieved from http://www.dlib.org/dlib/october00/10inbrief.html.

Open Source and Digital Repositories 73

9. Michel Castagné, "Institutional Repository Software Comparison: DSpace, EPrints, Digital Commons, Islandora, and Hydra," *University of British Columbia.* doi: http://dx.doi.org/10.14288/1.0075768.

10. "About Fedora," Duraspace, accessed July 25, 2020, https://duraspace.org/fedora/about/; "About Islandora," Lyrasis, accessed July 25, 2020, https://wiki.lyrasis.org/display/ ISLANDORA/About+Islandora#space-menu-link-content.

11. Jon Dunn and Richard Green, "The Samvera Community: An Overview," https://wiki.lyrasis.org/display/samvera/Samvera?preview=/87459292/181798489/The%20SamvSam%20Community_%20An%20Overview%20(2).pdf.

12. "Project," Omeka.org, accessed July 29, 2020, https://omeka.org/about/project/.

13. "OpenDOAR Home," Jisc Services Limited, accessed July 29, 2020, https://v2.sherpa.ac.uk/opendoar/.

14. Robert Tansley, Mick Bass, David Stuve, Margaret Branschofsky, Daniel Chudnov, Greg McClellan, and MacKenzie Smith, "The DSpace Institutional Digital Repository System: Current Functionality," *Proceedings of the 2003 Joint Conference on Digital Libraries* (2003): 87, http://hdl.handle.net/1721.1/26705.

15. "Technical Specifications," Duraspace.org, accessed July 25, 2020, https://duraspace.org/dspace/resources/technical-specifications/.

16. "Learn About LDAP," LDAP.com, accessed August 4, 2020, https://ldap.com/learn-about-ldap/; "How Shibboleth Works," Shibboleth.net, accessed August 4, 2020, https://www.shibboleth.net/index/basic/.

17. "Technical Specifications," Duraspace.org.

18. "Extensions and Addons Work," Lyrasis, updated January 15, 2019, https://wiki.lyrasis.org/display/DSPACE/Extensions+and+Addons+Work#ExtensionsandAddonsWork-AuthorityControl.

19. Duraspace.org, "LYRASIS and DuraSpace Complete Merger—Members and Community Benefit," July 9, 2019, https://duraspace.org/lyrasis-and-duraspace-complete-merger-members-and-community-benefit/.

20. "Features," Duraspace.org, accessed August 4, 2020, https://duraspace.org/dspacedirect/about/features/.

21. "About Us," 4Science, accessed August 4, 2020, https://www.4science.it/en/about-us/.

22. "Services," 4Science, accessed August 4, 2020, https://www.4science.it/en/services/.

23. "DSpace Express," Atmire.com, accessed August 4, 2020, https://www.atmire.com/dspace-express.

24. "Custom DSpace," Atmire.com, accessed August 4, 2020, https://www.atmire.com/custom-dspace.

25. "Services," The Library Code, accessed August 4, 2020, https://www.the-library-code.de/index.en.html.

26. "History," Eprints.org, updated September 8, 2017, http://wiki.eprints.org/w/History.

27. "Home," Cogprints Cognitive Sciences EPrint Archive, accessed July 29, 2020, http://cogprints.org/.

28. "EPrints Github Repository," GitHub, accessed July 29, 2020, https://github.com/eprints/eprints.

29. "History," Eprints.org.

30. "OpenDOAR," Jisc Services Limited, accessed July 29, 2020, https://v2.sherpa.ac.uk/cgi/search/repository/advanced?screen=Search&repository_name_merge=ALL&repository_name=&repository_org_name_merge=ALL&repository_org_name=&software_name=eprints&content_types_merge=ANY&content_subjects_merge=ANY&org_country_browse_merge=ALL&org_country_browse=&satisfyall=ALL&order=preferred_name&_action_search=Search.

31. Castagné, "Institutional Repository Software Comparison," 5.

32. "Wiki Home," Eprints.org, updated November 20, 2018, https://wiki.eprints.org/w/ Main_Page.

33. "How To," EPrints.org, updated June 15, 2012, https://wiki.eprints.org/w/Category:Howto; "Installation," updated May 19, 2020, https://wiki.eprints.org/w/Category:Installation; "Training Video," Eprints.org, updated May 17, 2018, "https://wiki.eprints.org/w/Category: Training_Video"; "Contact," EPrints.org, updated August 30, 2018, https://wiki.eprints.org/w/Contact.

34. Ibid.

35. "Frequently Asked Questions," Eprints.org, accessed July 29, 2020, https://www.eprints.org/services/ faq.php#q1.

36. Ibid.

37. "EPrints in the USA," Eprints.org, accessed July 29, 2020, https://www.eprints.org/us/eprints-in-the-usa/.

38. "History," EPrints Wiki, accessed July 29, 2020, https://wiki.eprints.org/w/History; "EPrints 3.4.2 Release Documentation," EPrints.org, accessed July 29, 2020, http://files.eprints.org/2500/.

39. Castagné, "Institutional Repository Software Comparison," 5; "OpenDOAR," Jisc Services Limited, accessed July 29, 2020, https://v2.sherpa.ac.uk/cgi/search/repository/ advanced?screen=Search&repository_name_merge=ALL&repository_name=&repository_org_name_merge=ALL&repository_org_name=&software_name=eprints&content_types_merge=ANY&content_subjects_merge=ANY&org_country_browse_merge=ALL&org_country_browse=&satisfyall=ALL&order=preferred_name&_action_search=Search.

40. Paul Pound and Melissa Anez, "Islandora Past, Present, and Future," Islandora Camp 2013, accessed August 4, 2020, https://islandora.ca/sites/default/files/Islandora%20Past%20Present%20and%20Future.pdf.

41. "Installations Map," Islandora.ca, accessed August 4, 2020, https://islandora.ca/installations-map.

42. "About Islandora," Islandora Wiki, updated August 20, 2015, https://wiki.lyrasis.org/display/ ISLANDORA/About+Islandora.

43. "About Islandora," Islandora Wiki.

44. "About," Drupal.org, accessed July 31, 2020, https://www.drupal.org/about.

45. "About," Drupal.org.

46. "Services," discoverygarden, Inc., accessed July 31, 2020, https://www.discoverygarden.ca/services.

47. "Open Repository Solutions," Born-Digital.com, accessed July 31, 2020, https://born-digital.com/islandora/.

48. "Service Companies," Islandora.ca, accessed July 31, 2020, https://islandora.ca/service-companies.

49. Chris Awre and Richard Green, "From Hydra to Samvera: An Open Source Community Journey," *Insights* 30, no. 3 (November 2017): 83, http://doi.org/10.1629/uksg.383.

50. Ibid.

51. Ibid.

52. "Samvera Implementations: In Production," Samvera Wiki, updated June 28, 2020, https://wiki.lyrasis.org/display/samvera/Samvera+Implementations%3A+In-production; "Samvera Implementations: In Development," Samvera Wiki, updated June 25, 2020, https://wiki.lyrasis.org/display/samvera/Samvera+Implementations%3A+In-development.

53. "Service Providers," Samvera, accessed August 1, 2020, https://samvera.org/getting-started/service-providers/.

54. "Platform," CoSector, accessed August 1, 2020, https://cosector.com/platform#samvera-hyrax-hosting; "Service Providers," Samvera.

55. "Services," Data Curation Experts, accessed August 1, 2020, https://curationexperts.com/services/.

56. "Discount Structure," Data Curation Experts, updated January 10, 2014, https://curationexperts.com/2014/01/10/2014-rate-sheet/.

57. "Samvera Digital Repository Solutions," Notch8, accessed August 1, 2020, https://www.notch8.com/samvera-digital-repository-solutions/.

58. "Ubiquity Repositories," Ubiquity Press, accessed August 1, 2020, https://u-repo.io.

59. This demo URL is for Omeka S. A sandbox environment used to exist for Omeka classic, but the link to it appears to be dead. Instead, if you wish to try Omeka classic, you can sign up for a free trial at https://www.omeka.net/signup.

5

Open Source Discovery

For the purposes of this chapter, library discovery systems will be used as a broad term for public-facing interfaces that expose a library's or another cultural organization's collection(s). Many different types of systems can fall under this category. Depending on the context, the user community, or the scale, they might be referred to as online public access catalogs (OPACs), catalogs, next-generation catalogs, extended OPACs, discovery interfaces, federated search, union catalogs, and/or web-scale discovery services.

Similar to digital repositories, the modern library discovery system is relatively new compared to the ILS and online databases. They also have a shared history in that much of their existence is owed to the shift to born-digital and electronic content from the pre-Internet, print-dominated world. In addition to their shared history, the discovery systems or back-end technologies for discovery discussed in this chapter are often a large piece of the public side of digital repositories covered in chapter 4 of this guide.

By 2010, all of the current OSS discovery systems we'll cover in this chapter existed in some form and have continued to evolve as user expectations change, as technologies shift and evolve, and as large vendors offer new web-scale discovery systems.

HISTORY AND CURRENT STATE

This is not a complete history of library discovery tools and methods but is instead intended to provide a brief overview of the library discovery interfaces since the age of automation. For the purposes of this chapter, starting with that history in the 1960s and sticking to a high-level view of the environment where possible is best. Like other library automation efforts that culminated in systems like the ILS, discovery systems represent several components of previous library or related systems.

The first of these components is online databases. From the middle of the 1960s to the early 1970s, there was a radical increase in the creation of databases, specifically word-oriented or bibliographic databases. These databases were subject databases and typically oriented around domains that relied on how quickly research could be put into practice and users being able and willing to pay for access such as science, commerce, and medical fields.[1] Due to the high cost and difficulty accessing these databases, academic libraries quickly became subscribers offering these databases as a service to their patrons for research purposes. As processing power increased and the earliest forms of the Internet and networked connections became available, online databases became more and more prevalent. In 1964, the precursor to MEDLINE (and PubMed), MEDLARS, became operational for batch searching.[2] In 1965, Chemical Abstracts Service's CBAC database became operational. At the time, there were estimated to be around twelve to twenty databases available. By 1970, there were between fifty to one hundred databases, including the Library of Congress MARC database in 1969 and the Ohio College Library Center (OCLC) shared cataloging systems in 1971 with fifty-four participating libraries. In 1980, there were over 600 databases. By this time, they were often referred to as online databases. Chemical Abstracts Service's CAS ONLINE and the NEXIS full-text database are examples of these databases. By 1985, over 6,000 libraries were OCLC members. To coincide with the expansion, OCLC changed its name in 1981 to Online Computer Library Center.[3] Many of these databases and services are still available and in high demand in 2020 though names have changed or they are part of a larger organization's content footprint. For example, many online databases are now available as part of subscription packages large content providers such as ProQuest and EBSCO now provide through partnerships or acquisition.

The next piece of our brief history is the Online Public Access Catalog (OPAC). The precursor to OPACs were card catalogs. As such, some of the early design models mimicked the card catalog while others relied on Boolean searching models favored by online databases such as Medline.[4] Breeding, in 2014, best summarized OPACs when he wrote the following: "[OPACs] provided an interface that could be used by library patrons to find materials owned by the library and managed in the ILS. Online catalogs were entirely integrated with the data structures of the ILS and provided the ability to search or browse the collection, to view an item's current location and availability status, and to perform requests such as requesting an item on loan to another borrower."[5]

While OPACs also date back to the 1960s, it wasn't until the 1980s when they became commonly available as part of the now mature, commercially viable ILS. Even though OPACs evolved over the years from a text-based terminal to a graphical user interface (GUI) and evolved to combine the two dominant query design models of card catalog and online database emulation, there was overall little change to the OPACs functionality or the content to which it provided access.[6] However, as internet access became more widespread, end-user expectations soared when comparing their library search experience to consumer search engine websites and Web 2.0 technologies.[7]

By the mid-2000s, there was widespread agreement from many librarians that the OPAC had failed as an adequate discovery tool for library users.[8] The lack of usability in navigating a library's collections online was seen as a major impediment for libraries in the early years of the twenty-first century in their ability to compete with emerging options available online.[9] At the heart of this argument was the idea that libraries were rapidly being left behind by Web 2.0 features and consumer search and retrieval sites such as Google and Amazon.[10] While vendors were slow to respond, libraries with easy access to OSS applications like the components of a LAMP server and search and index applications like Lucene and Solr were not.

WEB 2.0 AND NEXT GENERATION CATALOGS

At the heart, Web 2.0 represents the move from users being passive consumers online to the shift to a focus on the end-user ability to interact with content and with each other as well as the ability to create and easily share content.[11] Examples of Web 2.0 are user-generated content like media, reviews, comments, a focus on usability, and social media. In the early 2000s, librarians took heed of their patrons' expectations and, increasingly, their own expectations and began to identify the shortcomings of the current library discovery experience in library literature and conferences.[12] The solutions to many of these problems were based on Web 2.0 features and features commonly seen searching Amazon and Google. According to Breeding and others, the more popular proposed were single search, relevance ranking, facets, recommendations, and enriched records.[13]

The earliest next-generation OPAC projects introduced many of these features and were relatively fast to appear in response to the issues so many practitioners laid out. In 2005, North Carolina State University (NCSU) Libraries were the first library to deploy their own discovery system using Endeca—a commercial firm based in Cambridge, Massachusetts—taking the reins back from vendors in terms of library discovery systems.[14] Also starting in 2005, at the University of Virginia's (UVA) Libraries, Bethany Nowviskie shared her and Erik Hatcher's work on the OSS Collex tools that powers the NINES project (https://nines.org).[15] Collex led to the creation of the OSS Blacklight discovery system in 2007 at UVA Libraries.[16] That same year, the University of Rochester Library created Extensible Catalog, an early open source project incorporating Web 2.0 and library discovery wish list features. According to Mike Beccaria and Dan Scott in their article, "Fac-Back-OPAC: An Open Source Interface to Your Library System," the main theme of the 2007 Code4Lib conference was the open source search server Solr, including workshops and presentations by Erik Hatcher (Blacklight developer) and Andrew Nagy (VuFind developer).[17] Prior to VuFind's official release in 2010, in 2009, a fork of VuFind was already in development by Marmot Library Network for consortium and public library use that eventually would be known as Pika.[18]

Beginning in the 2010s, many of these features became commonplace, even in the native OPAC within certain ILSs, including Evergreen and Koha. What came to be known as web-scale discovery systems such as EBSCO Discovery Service (EDS), Ex Libris Primo, ProQuest Summon, and OCLC WorldCat Local (and later WorldCat Discovery) appeared as well and have, for the most part, taken all of these improvements to a new level by adding even more discoverability to their systems by introducing a central index or knowledge base where all of a library's content can be configured for ingestion. The result is a single search across hundreds or thousands of databases, journals, or other collections. These systems thus far have been marketed to and adopted by mostly academic libraries. While these systems represent a major advance, they are far from perfect. One of the more recent concerns has centered on search algorithms and relevancy ranking. Since these tools are proprietary, there has been some concern about the lack of transparency involved in determining what results are presented to a user. Some research even suggests these tools are algorithmically biased.[19] Another downside is the high maintenance cost incurred from maintaining the index or knowledge base pieces of these discovery systems. A discovery system is only as good as the metadata it ingests. Lastly, the costs of these systems are often significant, with limited customization and transparency in how they work. Perhaps because of the amount of maintenance involved with rapidly changing licensed content in an index or knowledge base, an OSS option has been elusive. However, the GOKb project (https://gokb.org/) aims to alleviate this issue by serving as an OSS knowledge base for various systems to tie into.[20] The amount of community involvement necessary to improve the value of GOKb, like any OSS project, will be significant, but an OSS alternative is very appealing to many. The OSS discovery options covered below have also come up with their own methods of coexisting with web-scale systems, either by specializing in unique or book-centric collections where web-scale systems fall short or treating web-scale like other integration opportunities and incorporating them into the OSS discovery system's results that many libraries have taken advantage of due to the customization of the discovery experience this makes possible.

OPEN SOURCE OPTIONS

Aspen Discovery

Community: https://bywatersolutions.com/projects/aspen-discovery
Code: https://github.com/mdnoble73/aspen-discovery
Live Demo: https://aspen-model.bywatersolutions.com/

Aspen Discovery is a continuation of the work Mark Noble and others at Marmot Library Network started in 2009 with Pika.[21] As a branch of an early version of VuFind, Aspen is licensed GPL v2.0. In late 2019, Noble's company, Turning Leaf, was acquired by ByWater Solutions, where Noble is now the Aspen Discovery Team Lead.[22] Though OSS discovery options have existed since the mid-2000s, Aspen Discovery is unique in that one of the largest commercial service providers specializing in open source library applications—ByWater Solutions—offers hosting, support, and development. Though less than a year old as of this writing, it has implementations already in place at several consortia in the United States, with dozens more due by the time this guide has likely gone to press.[23]

Background and Current State

Aspen is built on a LAMP stack architecture with the addition of Solr as the index engine for searching and browsing collections. It is based on the earliest versions of VuFind.[24] As the years have passed with any branch or fork, the systems bear little similarity with each other both on the front end and back end. The most significant changes, according to Noble, have been regarding the administration of Aspen.[25] Much of the configuration options were moved into the MySQL or MariaDB database rather than configuration files—often .ini files—on the server. Other features have been added to appeal to consortia or large networks of libraries, like the ability to configure settings based on the institution type. An example Noble provided was making configuration changes across all elementary schools rather than having to make changes individually for all elementary schools in a system with a shared catalog across a city or county school district.[26] Besides faceted searching, which allows a user to intuitively refine their search, relevancy, which uses various factors to weigh the importance of each title and represent them in the search results accordingly, and features available through integration with various ILSs like patron sign-in and item management, and item availability, Aspen also features what Noble refers to as "record grouping" where similar items are grouped for a more coherent search and results page experience. This is also referred to as FRBR (pronounced fur-burr) or FRBR-like, which stands for Functional Requirements for Bibliographic Records, and is a set of standards published in 1998 with the goal of improving the search experience by more naturally grouping results.[27]

Though many of the active sites are public or school libraries within consortia or networks, the integration of EDS into Aspen was recently completed and should appeal to academic libraries with options to customize display of those integrations.[28] Other integrations are widely available and in-demand by public libraries but also increasingly academic libraries as well. Examples include econtent providers like Overdrive, Hoopla, RBMedia, and NoveList for recommendations.[29] Enriched record views for each title level item as well as spelling correction and suggestions in search are also available.

Community and Service Providers

According to libraries.org, there are approximately 119 libraries that use Aspen, including branches using Aspen Discovery, with most being members of a consortium. The community is growing quickly for Aspen, and the pace of development is rapid, with releases happening every few weeks as of this writing. While the vast majority of that work is done by Noble, he noted an increasing number of developers becoming involved as more institutions with the necessary resources and expertise adopt the software. Nashville Public Library is a recent example of one such library system.

ByWater Solutions (https://bywatersolutions.com): With its ever-growing stake in the OSS library systems environment, ByWater acquiring Turning Leaf and Noble's expertise with OSS discovery aligns well with its other services and likely its long-term success. With ByWater able to offer hosting, support, and customized development to a discovery interface that is geared toward consortia and public libraries, this should allow ByWater to more directly compete with other service providers and other ILSs that have been successful with consortia and library networks. It is also likely that Aspen Discovery will be closely integrated with Koha and FOLIO in the future.

Future Outlook

Because of the concentration of development, hosting, and support resting on Noble and ByWater Solutions, much of Aspen's future could rely on ByWater's overall strategy. For any library looking for an affordable service provider with experience hosting, supporting, and developing a discovery platform that supports integration with many content providers and ILSs, Aspen Discovery hosted by ByWater is an attractive option. As more diverse libraries adopt Aspen, the community and participation will likely grow and with it perhaps other hosting options or sites hosting their own instances, as we see with Blacklight and VuFind. Mark Noble, the main developer of both Aspen and previously with Pika, has demonstrated what copyleft open source licenses make possible. By joining ByWater Solutions, Noble is potentially setting a new path for OSS discovery, forcing more and more libraries in the United States to look seriously at an OSS discovery option with hosting, support, and development being provided by an established and successful library services provider.

Blacklight

Community: https://projectblacklight.org
Code: https://github.com/projectblacklight/blacklight
Open Hub Profile: https://www.openhub.net/p/blacklight
Live Demo: https://demo.projectblacklight.org/

Officially released in 2009, Blacklight was originally developed by University of Virginia Libraries (UVA) and is available under a permissive Apache 2.0 license. It's a Ruby on Rails application that uses Solr as the search index.[30] It has been adopted by many for unique digital collection and digital library discovery as well as for large research academic library discovery interfaces such as Cornell, Penn State, and Indiana Universities. Echoing the stated needs of many practitioners in the mid-2000s, Blacklight's design goals, according to Elizabeth Sadler in 2009, were "relevance ranking, faceted browsing, open source design principles, the ability to include siloed materials, customizable interfaces for specific user populations, and re-mixable data."[31]

Background and Current State

Blacklight was built on top of Collex, which enabled "Web 2.0-inspiried interaction with federation online collections" for the Networked Infrastructure for Nineteenth-Century Electronic Scholarship, or NINES, project

Blacklight

Can you share the story of Blacklight at your organization?
At the United States Holocaust Memorial Museum, prior to the introduction of Blacklight, the Museum's web presence included separate web interfaces for photographs and for historical film and used a commercial library OPAC for published materials and a subset of the Museum's object and archival collections. The Office of Collections (now the National Institute for Holocaust Documentation [NIHD]) decided to investigate how to make the entire collection accessible. We decided that Museum collections of every type, including objects, archival collections, both large and small, historical films, oral histories, recorded sound, photographs, books, and other published materials, should all be searched together in one place—even though they are cataloged using various systems. The developers reviewed commercial software and other open source projects and selected open source systems due to the ability to perform deep customization in a highly agile fashion. Among the few viable open source projects at the time, Blacklight stood out largely because it was designed with few "opinions" concerning the format of data in the Solr index and because our catalog data formats varied across each type of collection. Using Blacklight as a cross-collection discovery system began as a "skunkworks" project in late 2010 on our intranet and became popular as more features and collections were added. It went live on the public web at the end of 2012. New features have been added, using agile approaches, and the site is now our "Collections Search," with over two million user sessions annually at the time of this writing. An intranet version is essentially identical but provides access to certain features and materials that cannot be shared on the web.

Because Blacklight is open source, we have been able to customize it to the extreme, adding features as our developer resources allow. It now has embedded streaming video and audio players; integration with our Digital Assets Management System; an implementation of the IIIF-based Universal Viewer for hierarchically arranged archival collections; embedded books from Internet Archive cataloged by our Library; integrations with reference request and collection request systems; searchable linked finding aids and page-level transcription text; and many other customized features that have been requested by museum staff. The site has been through two major redesigns, and we are continually adding new features and new integrations with other systems.

How would you describe the Blacklight community?
I first became aware of Blacklight through the Code4lib conference and Open Repositories conference. The Blacklight developer community has been unfailingly supportive, warm, welcoming, and very open to responding to questions or requests for assistance. My feeling is that Blacklight community participants enjoy working to aid in making collections discoverable and in helping one another.

How has Blacklight benefitted your organization?
As the collection has become more discoverable, the demand and use of the collection have increased. Users of every type, from exhibition designers to scholarly researchers and other people around the world, access our Collection descriptions and, in more and more cases, can interact with digitized materials from the Collection. Having every type of collection material discoverable and accessible in the same interface has helped to create a more cohesive culture within our institution, leading to closer collaboration in support of the museum's priority to ensure the accessibility of our collections.

Michael Levy
United States Holocaust Memorial Museum
Washington, DC

(https://nines.org) at the University of Virginia Libraries.[32] Also known as a UV-A light, a blacklight emits long-wave ultraviolet light and little actual visible light.[33] Nowviskie, Sadler, and Hatcher, in 2007, wrote that they chose the name for Blacklight for their prototype, "because it enhances the findability of 3.8 million UVA MARC records through a robust search-and-discovery."[34] They went on to write, "we like the Blacklight name because of the shift in perspective that comes about when work such as ours sheds a different light on familiar data and problem sets."[35]

As of this writing, the latest release from the prototype they developed in 2007 is version 7.10.0, and according to the repository on GitHub, it is the two-hundredth version release of Blacklight.[36] Blacklight's notable early adopters were UVA in 2008, Stanford in 2009, NCSU and University of Wisconsin–Madison in 2010. Early adopters also included prominent museums and archives such as the WGBH Open Vault, the Rock'n'Roll Hall of Fame, and the US Holocaust Museum. Today, this mix of museums, archives, and academic research libraries still reflects the overall Blacklight community.[37]

As noted, Blacklight's features include many of the desired features lobbied for by librarians in the mid-2000s during the Web 2.0 drive like faceting, relevancy, and recommendations. In addition to things that improve search experience, Blacklight features a few popular add-ons that better fit a certain institution's needs, such as Spotlight for digital collections, GeoBlacklight for geospatial data, ArcLight for archival materials, and Blacklight *MARC* for library bibliographic MARC records.[38] These add-ons create distinct flavors of Blacklight that better support the content and use cases of various Blacklight community members.

Community and Service Providers

The Blacklight community consists of academic libraries, museums, archives, and special collection projects. It's a diverse community, but many of these organizations have the funding and/or infrastructure in place to host and customize Blacklight to suit their needs. Based on libraries.org data, there are around forty-three libraries and their branches using Blacklight as their main discovery interface. This does not include the many other applications like Samvera and customized solutions where Blacklight serves as a front-end.

While there is an active community with high-profile ARL libraries participating in the project with diverse use cases, there are no dedicated and prominent service providers for Blacklight offering hosting, support, and custom development, though it is possible some of Samvera's service providers listed in chapter 4 of this guide might be willing and able to assist in development on a case-by-case basis. As a result, a site that would like to implement Blacklight should have the resources to host—either in a public or private cloud—support, and customize on their own.

Future Outlook

When discussing Blacklight's history in 2015, Robert Cartolano also discussed Blacklight's future in several areas: community, standards, search improvements and extension, and alternatives to Solr. More than any other OSS discovery system, Blacklight relies on a strong, collaborative community to make for a more sustainable and successful project as there are no service providers that can often play a large role in the governance and long-term strategy of these projects. Cartolano also advocates for adopting tools and standards to strengthen the project, like the International Image Interoperability Framework (IIIF), as well as prioritizing, improving, and extending search capabilities through responsive web design principles and accessibility. Cartolano advocates for work on the Hydra (now Samvera) project and add-ons/flavors previously mentioned like GeoBlacklight. Finally, Cartolano discusses a future beyond Solr where Elasticsearch and web-scale options are possible.[39]

Since that presentation at the 2015 Blacklight Summit, there have been many summits and two major version releases (6.x and 7.x). An option to support IIIF was developed and released in 2018. Blacklight is mobile device friendly and meets accessibility standards, and add-ons are highlighted on the main project page. There is still a way to go, but all of these improvements speak to the Blacklight community's strength and bright future.

Pika by Marmot Library Network

Project: https://www.marmot.org/pika-discovery/
Code: https://github.com/MarmotLibraryNetwork/Pika
Open Hub: https://www.openhub.net/p/vufind-plus
Live demo: https://opac.marmot.org/

A branch of VuFind, development started on Pika before VuFind 1.0 was officially released in 2010 to cater to the specific needs of the Marmot Library Network's member libraries where the shared ILS's OPAC in use by the consortium wasn't meeting the need.[40] As Marmot's official Pika site states, "Pika development started in 2009 based on an early version of VuFind... At that time, VuFind was primarily intended for use by academic libraries. Marmot added significant functionality intended to make VuFind more relevant to public libraries and more configurable for usage by a multi-type consortium."[41] As a branch of VuFind, it is a GPL v 2.0 licensed application, and with the addition of Solr, it relies on a LAMP stack server configuration.

Background and Current State

Pika's history on the Marmot Library Network website is well-documented. Development on Pika started in 2009 and continued to 2012, with member libraries such as Douglas County and Wake County Public Libraries assisting in development by adding significant new features like NoveList recommendations, custom recommendation functionality, development to support ebook purchasing models, item/title request functionality for items not owned by a library, and, in 2012, a new focus on usability for users and staff.[42] This included perhaps the biggest difference structurally between Pika (and Aspen) and VuFind: the administration interface developed to help individual libraries and consortia manage their collections and integrations in the discovery interface instead of flat configuration files where the application is installed.

In 2013, Marmot began working with "Discovery Partners." This model allowed Marmot to provide hosting and support services for Pika for libraries that were not interested or eligible to become members of Marmot. In 2014, this branch of VuFind, called VuFind Plus, was named Pika to avoid confusion. This change was part of a major update that included the FRBR-like "Record Grouping to allow all formats and editions of a work to be grouped together to help users easily identify which formats are available," as well as responsive design and browse features.[43] In 2015, Nashville Public Library with Metropolitan Nashville Public Schools became a Discovery Partner to integrate their school and branch catalogs into one integrated experience for the Limitless Libraries program.[44]

Pika, in its ten-year-plus history, has demonstrated that there is a need and demand for open source discovery interfaces for public and school libraries as well as consortia.

Community and Service Providers

According to libraries.org, approximately 430 libraries and their branches use Pika. A large percentage of that number is composed of the Mesa County School District in Colorado and the Metropolitan Nashville Public School System in Nashville, Tennessee, as well as the Nashville Public Library (NPL) and its branches.

Marmot Library Network (https://www.marmot.org/): For development, hosting, and support of Pika, a library does not need to be a full member of Marmot Library Network, which focuses on libraries within the US State of Colorado offering not just Pika but the Sierra ILS as well. Libraries wishing to use Pika in a hosted environment can become Discovery Partners with Marmot.

Future Outlook

Pika's future in the short term is one of continued success, but a recent white paper published by the Marmot Library Network marks a move towards more investment in FOLIO and other OSS ILSs like Evergreen and Koha as replacements to IIIF's Sierra ILS. The paper also includes plans for implementing and hosting VuFind.[45] Both of these activities will appeal to academic libraries. It is difficult to predict how this will impact Pika in the long term, but Marmot supporting multiple discovery interfaces could require more resources for development, maintenance, and support. Because of how diverse and comparatively large the VuFind community is around the globe, Pika could be at a disadvantage.

VuFind

>Community: https://VuFind.org/VuFind/
>Code: https://github.com/VuFind-org/VuFind
>Open Hub Profile: https://www.openhub.net/p/vufind
>Live Demo (or example): https://VuFind.org/demo/

VuFind is developed and maintained by Villanova University's Library.[46] Version 1.0 was released in 2010 under the copyleft GPL v 2.0 license. Of all OSS discovery systems, it likely has the largest international presence. VuFind's codebase is in PHP using Solr as a search and index application. Its architecture relies on a traditional LAMP stack server setup with the addition of Solr's Java dependencies.

Background and Current State

Though version 1.0 was released in 2010 under the copyleft GPL v 2.0 license, VuFind's earliest beginnings date back to 2006, when it was originally developed by Andrew Nagy at Villanova University.[47] Nagy would go on to work to help develop Summon and FOLIO at Serials Solutions/ProQuest and EBSCO, respectively, but Villanova's Falvey Memorial Library continues to be heavily involved with VuFind development with Demian Katz as the lead developer of the project.[48] The beta period of VuFind lasted from 2007 to 2010, with version 2.0 arriving in 2013. Houser wrote in 2009 that the inspiration came from NCSU's work on Endeca though that solution was considered too costly for Villanova, so Nagy proposed a similar solution based on open source applications like Lucene and Solr.[49] The first prototype shown was dubbed MyResource portal at the Code4Lib 2007 Conference.[50] There was broad interest in VuFind from a range of libraries and consortia. In fact, despite developing VuFind, Villanova was the third library to go live as the National Library of Australia implemented in May 2008 and was followed by Minnesota State College and Universities just before Villanova in August 2008.[51]

The design goals for VuFind were much the same as Blacklight and other next-generation systems: single search similar to consumer search engines; faceted browsing and narrowing of results; enhanced records like book jackets and book reviews; persistent URLs; relevancy; recommendations; and the

VuFind

Can you share the story of VuFind at your organization?
After successfully evaluating VuFind as a discovery search system in 2011 at the Leipzig University Library, the project finc (find in catalog; https://finc.info) got funded by the European Union through the EFRE program to bring VuFind catalogs to eleven university libraries in Saxony, Germany. As a result of its success, the finc community got founded in the final stage of the project and guaranteed since then the maintenance and development of the VuFind-based finc catalogs. The finc community has grown to become nationwide, with more than twenty members.

How would you describe the VuFind community?
The VuFind community, and especially its central person, Demian Katz, has been very supportive since our first steps with VuFind. Communication on the mailing list is very welcoming, responsive, productive, and professional. As open source software depends heavily on an active community, VuFind is a great example of a healthy project for more than a decade, and we are glad to be a part of it. In this regard, active participation and contribution are not limited by contributing code—the international VuFind community keeps growing and is sharing and discussing ideas on how to improve library catalogs for our patrons and librarians.

How has VuFind benefitted your organization?
The VuFind-centered finc project at Leipzig University Library proofed and established the productive use of infrastructure components based on open source software. In order to meet the needs of each library, the VuFind codebase had to be customized during the project. The development in terms of personal resources and the design of appropriate processes laid the foundation at Leipzig University Library to extend the use of open source software in its infrastructure and get engaged with other open source software communities resulting in the current active participation in the FOLIO project as developer and early adopter. Overall open source software enables us as organization to shape our IT infrastructure to our needs—regardless if the needs originate from our organizational requirements or the needs of our patrons.

André Lahmann
Leipzig University
Leipzig, Germany

ability to index from multiple sources and different data types such as records from IRs, DAMs, and MARC records.⁵²

Including the initial release, there have been seven major releases, with the latest version being version 7.0, released in July 2020. As other libraries have implemented VuFind, contributions have come in for more integration with other library systems, more enriched data options, and more modern styling templates. The latest release features new or improved integration for FOLIO, Koha, ArchivesSpace, and EDS.⁵³

Community and Service Providers

VuFind.org's installation page lists more than 200 institutions, mostly in North America and Europe.⁵⁴ Libraries.org lists approximately 750 libraries, consisting of their branches using it as their discovery interface, including large systems in the United States like the National Park Service, The Carnegie Library of Pittsburgh, and The Free Library of Philadelphia.⁵⁵

As far as service providers go, in stark contrast to the other OSS options discussed in this chapter, there are over a dozen support providers for VuFind listed at the VuFind.org site (https://vufind.org/vufind/support.html), with the vast majority based outside the United States. What follows is a list of all service providers the authors could confirm through each company's web presence that offer VuFind support, hosting, and development or some combination of these services.

allegronet.de (http://portal.allegronet.de/): Based in Germany, the VuFind support page indicates they offer web hosting for libraries, including VuFind as a Web 2.0 option.⁵⁶

Andornot Consulting (https://www.andornot.com): Based in Vancouver, British Columbia, Andornot Consulting offers VuFind as well as other systems like Omeka and the CORAL ERM to libraries and other cultural institutions.

DataScouting (https://datascouting.com/libraries-archives-museums/): Based in Greece and serving Europe, the Middle East and North Africa, and Latin America, DataScouting offers several services for OSS ILSs, IR, CMSs, as well as VuFind, which they refer to as a meta-search engine for libraries, archives, and museums as well as other industries.

effective WEBWORK (https://www.effective-webwork.de/): Based in Hamburg, Germany, effective WEBWORK offers software services for a number of OSS applications, including DSpace, FOLIO, and VuFind. Their website mentions they are development partners for two forks of VuFind—"beluga core" and "finc"—and demonstrate they are involved with the general VuFind community with their recent organizing of the VuFind user meeting 2019 in Hamburg.⁵⁷

iZi Software (http://www.izi.my/): Based in Malaysia and serving the region, iZi Software Solutions has been specializing in library information systems since 2003 and OSS development since 2009. According to their site, they provide installation, data migration, support, training, implementation, consultancy, hosting, and customization for Koha, DSpace, EPrints, and VuFind.

KnowledgeWARE Technologies (http://www.kwareict.com/en): Based in Saudi Arabia with a presence in many other countries in the region, KnowledgeWARE, or Kware technologies, describes itself as "a pan Arab systems integration firm which specializes in Bilingual (Arabic/English) Information Access Technology (IAT) based solutions for government agencies and commercial corporations. Kware founders have expertise in systems Arabization, virtual library information networks, intelligent search and retrieval tools, enterprise applications development and deployment, electronic databases access, knowledge management, document imaging and document capturing, and have successfully provided technical support and integration services for hundreds of commercial and government clients."[58] Library Systems services include Koha, DSpace, SubjectsPlus, and VuFind.

MMK GmbH (https://www.mmk-hagen.de/web-anwendungen/vufind-discovery-system.html): Based in Hagen, Germany, MMK GmbH provides a range of varied web services related to online commerce, e-learning, and content management systems as well as VuFind.

Open Geek Service (http://www.opengeekservice.cl/): based in Chile, Open Geek provides hosting, support, and customization services for VuFind, Koha, OJS, and DSpace throughout Latin America.

Orex (https://www.orex.es/vufind/): Based in Spain, Orex offers hosting and support services for Omeka, Koha, Bokeh, and VuFind.

outermedia (http://www.outermedia.de/): Based in Berlin, outermedia's site states they offer a customized version of VuFind addressing a particular institution's needs from libraries, archives, museums, and other cultural organizations.

PTFS Europe (http://www.ptfs-europe.com/): Based out of the United Kingdom and previously discussed in chapter 3 of this guide, PTFS Europe provides implementation services, development, and training for several OSS products, including VuFind.

Scanbit (http://www.scanbit.net/): Based in Spain, Scanbit offers support and hosting services for a number of OSS library applications, including VuFind.

Tamil (http://www.tamil.fr/): Based in Paris, Tamil offers a range of hosting and support services for VuFind as well as Koha.

Xercode (http://www.xercode.es/): Based in Spain, Xercode offers services for a number of library OSS applications, including VuFind.

Future Outlook

Recent work to integrate VuFind with FOLIO may be a sign of things accelerating for the VuFind project. Simmons University in Boston, Massachusetts, just announced their successful implementation of FOLIO with VuFind acting as its catalog. Using VuFind as the front-end discovery layer along with FOLIO (and Project Reshare discussed in chapter 6 of this guide) could lead to it being in some way bundled with FOLIO by vendors implementing, hosting, and supporting FOLIO in the future.

As already discussed, the latest main release of VuFind as of July 2020 is version 7. The iterative improvements between version 1 in 2010 and version 7 are impressive, with integration support for importing records from multiple ILSs and other types of systems. There has also been increased interest from libraries working to integrate VuFind and FOLIO since FOLIO has no native discovery component.

SUMMARY

OSS discovery is still a new and developing world and is still a rather small one. VuFind and branches of it represent the majority of OSS discovery options available today. Solr is the search and browse application of choice, though if a branch of an existing system or new discovery system appeared using Elasticsearch—the index engine used by Koha's and Invenio's OPAC discussed in chapter 3—it would not be surprising.[59] As we've seen with other OSS library systems discussed throughout this guide, hosting and support providers often play a critical role in guiding an OSS application's development and fostering its community. Blacklight stands out as an exception with no official service providers but instead consists of a tight-knit community of research libraries, archives, and museums.

Depending on the type of library and their needs, one or more of these systems will meet the need and allow a degree of freedom for customization not possible otherwise. Many of the challenges and needs laid out by librarians and technologists in the mid-2000s have been realized by the options covered in this chapter. These systems now must evolve in response to web-scale discovery services and library services platforms becoming more and more commonplace. How OSS options decide to get along with these services or offer their own alternatives will be worth following.

NOTES

1. M. Lynne Neufeld and Martha Cornog, "Database history: From dinosaurs to compact discs," *Journal of the American Society for Information Science* (July 1986): 183.

2. Batch searching was the process of using multiple search strategies when access and time available to search older databases were limited and/or costly. See Neufeld and Cornog, "Database history: From dinosaurs to compact discs."

3. Neufeld and Cornog, 189.

4. Christine L. Borgman, "Why Are Online Catalogs Still Hard to Use?," *Journal of the American Society for Information Science* (1996): 493.

5. Marshall Breeding, "Library Resource Discovery Products: Context, Library Perspectives, and Vendor Positions," *Library Technology Reports* (2014): 7.

6. Borgman, "Why Are Online Catalogs Still Hard to Use?," 493; Breeding, "Library Resource Discovery Products," 7–8.

7. "Web 2.0 refers to websites that emphasize user-generated content, ease of use, participatory culture and interoperability (i.e., compatible with other products, systems, and devices) for end users. The term was invented by Darcy DiNucci in 1999 and later popularized by Tim O'Reilly and Dale Dougherty at the O'Reilly Media Web 2.0 Conference in late 2004." *Wikipedia,* accessed May 5, 2020, https://en.wikipedia.org/wiki/Web_2.0.

8. Karen Schidner, "How OPACs Suck, Part 1: Relevance Rank (Or the Lack of It)," *American Library Association*, March 13, 2006; Karen Schidner, "How OPACs Suck, Part 2: The Checklist of Shame," *American Library Association*, April 3, 2006; Karen Schidner, "How OPACs Suck, Part 3: The Big Picture," *American Library Association*, May 20, 2006.

9. Jia Mi and Cathy Weng, "Revitalizing the library OPAC: Interface, Searching, and Display Challenges," *Information Technology and Libraries* (2008): 5–22. https://doi.org/10.6017/ital.v27i1.3259.

10. John Houser, "The VuFind Implementation at Villanova University," *Library Hi Tech*, (2009): 95. doi:10.1108/07378830910942955.

11. Marshall Breeding, "Next-Generation Library Catalogs," *Library Technology Reports*, (2007): 13–14. Summary from the Wikipedia Entry on Web 2.0, https://en.wikipedia.org/wiki/Web_2.0.

12. Mi and Weng, "Revitalizing the library OPAC"; Schidner, "How OPACs Suck."

13. Breeding, "Library Resource Discovery Products"; Houser, "The VuFind Implementation at Villanova University"; Elizabeth Sadler, "Project Blacklight: a next generation library catalog at a first generation university," *Library Hi Tech* 27, no. 1 (2006): 57–67, https://doi.org/10.1108/07378830910942919; Schidner, "How OPACs Suck."

14. Houser, "The VuFind Implementation," 95; NCSU information on Endeca catalog release: https://www.lib.ncsu.edu/endeca/.

15. Bethany Nowviskie, "COLLEX: semantic collections & exhibits for the remixable web," (November 2005), accessed July 30, 2020, https://nines.org/about/wp-content/uploads/2011/12/Nowviskie-Collex.pdf.

16. Bethany Nowviskie, Elizabeth Sadler, and Erik Hatcher, "Adapting an Open-Source Scholarly Web 2.0 System for Findability in Library Collections or: Frankly, Vendors, We Don't Give a Damn," *Library 2.0 initiatives in academic libraries* (Chicago: Association of College and Research Libraries, 2007), 59–72, accessed August 2, 2020, https://archive.org/details/library20initiat0000unse/page/58/mode/2up.

17. Mike Beccaria and Dan Scott, "Fac-Back-OPAC: An Open Source Interface to Your Library System," *Computers in Libraries*, October 2007, Accessed July 15, 2020, https://www.infotoday.com/cilmag/oct07/Beccaria_Scott.shtml.

18. Mark Noble, interview by author. Video recording. August 5, 2020.

19. For more reading on the subject of algorithm bias, see Safiya Umoja Noble, *Algorithms of Oppression: How Search Engines Reinforce Racism* (New York: New York University Press, 2018) and Matthew Reidsma, *Masked by Trust: Bias in Library Discovery* (Sacramento, CA: Litwin Books, 2019).

20. See https://gokb.org/about-gokb/ for more information about the GoKB OSS project.

21. Noble, interview by author.

22. Marshall Breeding, "Bywater Expands Support Offerings to Include Aspen Discovery," *Smart Libraries Newsletter* 39, no. 12 (2009): 4–5, accessed August 3, 2020, https://librarytechnology.org/document/24782.

23. Noble, Interview by author.

24. Ibid.

25. Ibid.

26. Ibid.

27. For more information on FRBR, see Olivia Madison, "The IFLA Functional Requirements for Bibliographic Records," *Library Resources & Technical Services* 44, no. 3 (July 2000): 153–59. doi:10.5860/lrts.44n3.15.

28. Noble, interview by author.

29. From ByWater's project page for Aspen Discovery. Accessed August 4, 2020, https://bywatersolutions.com/projects/aspen-discovery.

30. Project Blacklight, accessed July 15, 2020, http://projectblacklight.org; Official Ruby on Rails website, https://rubyonrails.org.

31. Sadler, "Project Blacklight: a next generation library catalog at a first generation university," 62.

32. Nowviskie, "Adapting an Open-Source Scholarly Web 2.0 System," 58.

33. Definition from Wikipedia, accessed July 17, 2020, https://en.wikipedia.org/wiki/Blacklight.

34. Nowviskie, "Adapting an Open-Source Scholarly Web 2.0 System," 61.

35. Ibid.

36. Blacklight release page, accessed July 20, 2020, https://github.com/projectblacklight/blacklight/releases.

37. Blacklight example page, accessed July 20, 2020, http://projectblacklight.org/#examples.

38. Blacklight Add-ons page, accessed July 20, 2020, https://github.com/projectblacklight/blacklight/wiki/Blacklight-Add-ons.

39. Robert Cartolano, "History of Blacklight," Academic Commons (2015), accessed July 21, 2020, https://academiccommons.columbia.edu/doi/10.7916/D8J38S9M.

40. "About Pika," accessed August 1, 2020, https://www.marmot.org/pika-discovery/about-pika.

41. Ibid.

42. Ibid.

43. Ibid.

44. Ibid. More information on Limitless Libraries can be found at http://limitlesslibraries.org.

45. "360 Evaluation Study & Results," accessed August 2, 2020, https://www.marmot.org/about/governance/council_and_executive_board.

46. Vufind.org, accessed July 23, 2020, https://vufind.org/vufind.

47. Houser, "The VuFind Implementation," 95; Profile on Andrew Nagy, accessed August 12, 2020, http://niso.org/people/andrew-nagy.

48. Breeding, "Library Resource Discovery Products," 49–50.

49. Houser, "The VuFind Implementation," 93.

50. Ibid. | Beccaria, "Fac-Back-OPAC."

51. Ibid.

52. Ibid.

53. VuFind Change Log, accessed August 10, 2020, https://vufind.org/wiki/changelog#release_70_-_7_20_2020.

54. "VuFind Customer Installations," accessed on August 1, 2020, https://VuFind.org/wiki/community:installations.

55. Libraries.org advanced search, accessed on August 1, 2020, https://librarytechnology.org/libraries/advanced.

56. "Community Support," accessed on July 31, 2020, https://vufind.org/vufind/support.html.

57. "Discovery-Systeme mit VuFind," accessed on August 1, 2020, https://www.effective-webwork.de/loesungen-tools/vufind/.

58. "About KnowledgeWARE," accessed on August 2, 2020, http://www.kwareict.com/en/node/102.

59. "Elasticsearch," accessed on August 13, 2020, https://www.elastic.co/elasticsearch.

6

Open Source Resource Sharing

Resource sharing between libraries has a long history and involves the loaning of items, digital and physical, to other libraries in a group, consortium, region, country, and beyond under typical library loan periods. This is commonly referred to as interlibrary loan (ILL), especially in reference to physical materials, and sometimes document delivery when referring to digital materials. Though often a niche of a library's access services operations, ILL, in recent years, has become crucial as libraries, especially academic, have begun to slim down their print collections to utilize the physical library spaces and budget to serve patrons in other ways. At the same time, licensing and technical challenges in resource sharing of digital-born content like electronic articles and books have put additional strain on lending libraries complying with and keeping track of copyright and licensing agreements from vendors. The software necessary to offer these services and within compliance of legal constraints increasingly must be weighed against cost and use. As a result, when looking at new systems and services for resource sharing, increasingly, libraries must review OSS options.

HISTORY AND CURRENT STATE

The history and current state of resource sharing revolve around the massive resource sharing star at its center, OCLC.[1] OCLC, which manages the global bibliographic database WorldCat, launched its first resource sharing service in 1979.[2] Among cataloging and metadata services, resource sharing products and services have been a core service of OCLC ever since, and OCLC's ILL services use of WorldCat has allowed OCLC to dominate the arena for many years.[3] Through the acquisition of competitors and their technologies, close partnerships with software providers, and the WorldCat database, OCLC has been very effective at providing consortia, regional, national, and even international ILL services for member libraries subscribing to their services.

The biggest challenge of traditional resource sharing in libraries is the task of a library to find the resource a patron needs, confirm which libraries hold it, come to an agreement with the selected lending library to send, confirm which borrowing library will receive it, and, finally, the return of the resource. Traditionally, it is the heart of how the service works, and nearly every resource sharing library system is designed around these workflows.[4] Because of the size of the WorldCat database and the number of libraries that OCLC members are using and regularly submitting updates of their library holdings to WorldCat, OCLC has consistently and successfully designed their resource sharing products around WorldCat. Because no other resource such as WorldCat exists, alternative library resource sharing systems have historically been at a disadvantage, and as of this writing, nearly every major resource sharing system has now been acquired by OCLC-owned or ProQuest-owned companies.[5] Today, OCLC provides multiple types of resource sharing products, including Relais, WorldShare ILL, Tipasa, and in partnership with Atlas Systems, ILLiad.

In 2008 Relais International announced it would release resource sharing software on an open source license.[6] That never came to pass, but Relais International products did emphasize the use of many open protocol standards such as ISO ILL, NCIP, and OpenURL, as well as open APIs and Z39.50, the workhorse standard. Relais was also an early pioneer in moving away from Windows OS-reliant client-server architecture to web-based options as well as vendor-hosted models.[7] They also worked successfully with OCLC, including access via Z39.50 to WorldCat and obtaining access to OCLC's ILL and WorldCat APIs that their users could use with the appropriate OCLC subscriptions.[8] However, despite the cooperation, OCLC and Relais were competitors, and in 2017, Relais was acquired by OCLC.[9] This acquisition occurred the same year OCLC released its cloud-based replacement for ILLiad, a more robust version of WorldShare ILL, Tipasa.[10]

Outside of OCLC's resource sharing options, there are others, but as noted earlier, they are typically more limited in their scope since no union catalog or consortium can currently match holdings and the resulting lending and borrowing options in WorldCat. Among alternative services is Innovative Interface's INN-Reach service. As Innovative was recently acquired by ProQuest, it will be interesting to see if there is more collaboration and work to extend INN-Reach services to Ex Libris library systems like Alma or integration with RapidILL services.

RapidILL, acquired by Ex Libris in 2019, was originally a dedicated journal article-lending service but began including physical item lending and borrowing, increasingly referred to as returnables, in 2014.[11] RapidILL was started by Colorado State University in 1997 after flooding damaged the library's serials collections.[12] At the time of acquisition by Ex Libris, there were several products available by RapidILL, including systems that focused on returnables like RapidILL's RapidR service.

As the biggest challenge to resource sharing systems has been interoperability between systems, a number of protocols exist to deal with these. Most notable are NCIP or NISO Circulation Interchange Protocol, ISO ILL, and the previously mentioned Z39.50. NCIP is utilized in a myriad of ways, from tying together disparate ILSs in exchanging patron, loan, and item info between sharing libraries to adding functionality to ILSs.[13] Auto-Graphics's SHAREit has been successful at demonstrating interoperability success by making possible union catalogs for large sharing groups like the Commonwealth Catalog system in Massachusetts, with NCIP and Z39.50 doing most of the heavy lifting. Also, of note outside of the OSS options listed in more detail in the sections that follow is the OSS ILS Koha; it has recently introduced ILL functionality for use between Koha libraries.[14]

Overall, the history and current state of resource sharing in libraries have consisted of two themes that sometimes overlap: striving for open standards and interoperability between disparate library systems and consolidation. Depending on their success and adoption, OSS alternatives could disrupt the latter theme while pushing forward the former further than has previously been possible.

OPEN SOURCE OPTIONS

FulfILLment

Project: http://fulfillment-ill.org/
Code: Contact Equinox
Demo: Contact Equinox

FulfILLment is a GPL-licensed software project initiated by OHIONET and developed by Equinox Software. According to the Equinox community page on FulfILLment, the architecture and business logic of the FulfILLment application plays to scaling the strengths of the Evergreen ILS.[15] To add to that, according to the FulfILLment site (http://fulfillment-ill.org), "this project has shown that there is a way to join the useful capabilities of consortial and scalable attributes of Evergreen with connectors to disparate ILSes in order to have a truly unmediated ILL process."[16]

Background and Current State

The FulfILLment project was started in 2009 when Equinox Software was awarded the contract for the development of an open source resource sharing application. Equinox built FulfILLment on the same strengths of Evergreen in its flexibility with large consortia. The original project was completed in late 2012, and at that time, it was being evaluated by a few libraries in California.

FulfILLment uses NCIP and Z39.50 in the same ways as other resource sharing applications do that are covered in this chapter. It also utilizes a union catalog in making resource discovery and requesting possible. Its strength is the LAIConnector or Local Automation Integrator. Based on the documentation:

> The LAIConnector is a tool for facilitating the sharing of information between disparate library systems. It was created to help aid in speeding the development of custom ILS connectors with the DRY or don't repeat yourself software engineering principle in mind. It is written in Perl, meant to be highly portable and essentially sits "on top" of your existing ILS and RESTfully facilitates communication with other systems via your web server.[17]

As FulfILLment is based largely on Evergreen, FulfILLment can utilize Equinox's Sequoia platform to integrate for hosting and implementation. Recently, the development priorities of FulfILLment have been focused around refreshing the entire code base with the latest versions and functionality of Evergreen. This includes search improvements, web-based functionality, and integration, allowing for more patron-initiated requests instead of staff-mediated ILL workflows. This also means developing more collaborative relationships with other systems to increase LAIConnector options.

Community and Service Providers

While the FulfILLment project was led by OHIONET with Equinox responsible for the development of the application, there were other organizations funding the project as well at the state library level.[18] The official FulfILLment project page and the Equinox site do not go into detail on organizations using FulfILLment, but in fact, approximately 225 libraries are using FulfILLment as part of the FindIT CT statewide library catalog.[19]

Equinox (https://www.equinoxinitiative.org/): Born from and made up of the developers who created the Evergreen ILS, Equinox Initiatives was originally founded in 2007. While they specialize in support, hosting, and development for Evergreen as well as Koha, they are the original developers of FulfILLment. Unique to Equinox is the Sequoia platform that these applications sit on, allowing for quick deployment, scalability, and stability.

Future Outlook

With the project website, code repository, and email lists having no new activity since early 2015, as of this writing, use of fulfILLment appears to be limited outside of findIT CT. However, recent development work to improve the search functionality and gear it towards a mostly patron-initiated application should allow it to directly compete with comparable resource sharing systems in the near future, especially systems like SHAREit, INN-Reach, and ReShare Returnables. Until the code, a live demo, and up-to-date documentation are available, it will be difficult for any individual library or group to review FulfILLment's viability for resource sharing or what development would be needed to suit an organization's unique needs. Future development of FulfILLment will rely largely on Equinox's work on increasing interoperability between ILSs with FulfILLment and bringing the recent improvements to Evergreen to the FulfILLment project.

Project ReShare

>Project: https://projectreshare.org/
>Code: https://github.com/openlibraryenvironment
>Demo: https://projectreshare.org/products/product-demo

"ReShare is an open-source, community-owned resource sharing platform currently being developed under the auspices of the Open Library Foundation (OLF)."[20] Potentially introducing the most disruption ever seen in the resource sharing arena, Project ReShare has several OSS products in development that could be serious competitors to the largest systems and services in the resource sharing environment. However, this all depends on participants and the momentum it is able to generate due to early successes. Project ReShare is licensed under an Apache 2.0 permissive license and relies on much of the same architecture and governance of the FOLIO project.[21]

Background and Current State

In 2020, Kristen Wilson of IndexData and Jill Morris of the Pennsylvania Academic Library Consortium, Inc. (PALCI) provided great detail on the motivation behind Project ReShare and inner workings of the governance structure under the OLF and types of products and services Project ReShare hopes to create by authoring a *Serials Librarian* article, "Project ReShare: Building a Community-Owned Resource Sharing Platform." While other consortia and libraries are involved in Project ReShare, Wilson and Morris illustrate PALCI's work in 2017 regarding concerns with their resource sharing environment and how sustainable that environment might be.[22] Perhaps most notably, the working group formed in 2017 had concerns regarding PALCI's resource sharing services in use—Relais D2D and RapidILL RapidR—especially when considering the long-term viability of the products themselves and future operability of services as both products were acquired by competing vendors—OCLC and Ex Libris, respectively.[23]

According to the product page of the Project ReShare website (https://projectreshare.org/products/), there are four products in various stages of development: ReShare Returnables, ReShare Shared Inventory, ReShare Controlled Digital Lending, and ReShare Non-Returnables. ReShare Returnables is focused on traditional print collection lending and borrowing functionality. ReShare Returnables might be best compared to Tipasa, SHAREit, or RapidILL's RapidR service. The Alpha release was on January 31, 2020, the Beta was on April 30, 2020, and ReShare Returnables version 1.0 was released on July 31, 2020.[24] Version 1.0 was the MVP, or minimal viable product, release for ReShare Returnables.[25] The MVP details were one of two outcomes when libraries and other stakeholders met in August 2018.[26] The other outcome was the model for community ownership detailed below.[27] The release of the MVP version 1.0 within two years after the community was first created is significant. It will be worth watching how closely future releases match up against the roadmap for future releases available on the Returnables product page (https://projectreshare.org/products/returnables/).

ReShare Shared Inventory is a shared catalog meant to provide a library group, network, and consortia with a common catalog to identify resources for lending and borrowing. VuFind, the OSS discovery layer, has been modified to support this type of shared catalog. Much like OCLC's GreenGlass product and use of WorldCat holdings, Wilson and Morris write, "The shared index may be harnessed for purposes that go beyond traditional resource sharing, such as collection analytics or management of a shared print repository."[28] VuFind has demonstrated it can handle many millions of bibliographic records at large universities like the University of Chicago and other sites.[29] The ReShare Shared Inventory and work being done in regards to FOLIO will present further evidence of VuFind and Solr's robustness.

The details and MVP requirements of ReShare Controlled Digital Lending are still in the works.[30] According to the product page, "Controlled digital lending (CDL) is the process of digitizing a physical item, making it inaccessible [to unauthorized users for copyright purposes], and lending a secure electronic copy in its place."[31] This brief description of the workflow is similar to the document delivery workflows in use by other systems, such as OCLC's Article Exchange service, which ties into resource sharing applications like ILLiad, WorldShare ILL, and Tipasa via API or OCLC authorization configuration, where access to the item expires after thirty days or five access attempts.[32] According to the CDL product website, MVP requirements will be determined in the winter of 2020, with several additional meetings to discuss additional functionality.

ReShare Non-Returnables is the fourth and final product part of Project ReShare. The MVP requirements were finalized in November 2019, but development has not started on Non-Returnables. According to the product page, it seems much of the Non-Returnables functionality will be included as part of the Returnables application:

> ReShare Non-Returnables will support the lending of articles, book chapters, and other portions of whole works that can be supplied via electronic delivery. Specific features identified for Non-Returnables include storage of print and electronic serial holdings in the Shared Inventory, copyright clearance management, and document storage and delivery. Many aspects of the existing ReShare Returnables product will be extended to support non-returnables, including load balancing algorithms, ISO 18626 messaging, and interoperability with local library management systems.[33]

All of the ReShare products use NCIP and Z39.50 standards for interoperability as well as the ISO 18626 standards for ILL messaging.

Community and Service Providers

The ReShare community at this point in time in the development of the ReShare products might be best summed up by the stakeholders and sponsors at the August 2018 member that commenced Project ReShare. That group consisted of stakeholders from PALCI, IndexData, Mozilla Foundation, the Open Library Foundation (OLF), the Triangle Research Libraries Network (TRLN), the Greater Western Library Alliance (GWLA), the Big Ten Academic Alliance (BTAA), and the Ivy Plus Libraries Confederation (IPLC) as the official Project ReShare site does not list individual, consortia, or commercial members.[34] In addition to these original project stakeholders, a recent news release welcomed Lehigh and Grand Valley State University as founding members of Project ReShare.[35]

Wilson and Morris also well-document the community ownership model ReShare uses. The OLF is the "legal home of the project and copyright owner for any software it produces," and all ReShare products are licensed under the Apache 2.0 permissive license.[36] There is also a well-defined project structure for the overall governance of ReShare. On top of the software developers, there are the SMEs, or subject matter experts, ensuring the detailed workflows are correct, the product managers are looking at the big picture of the products, and the steering committee is providing overall leadership and resources.[37]

As already mentioned, the project site does not specify who commercial members of Project ReShare are. However, IndexData is the lead developer of ReShare, much like the FOLIO project. As IndexData is entering the hosting and support market for FOLIO, it is likely IndexData is pursuing this path as well for ReShare. There is also a high likelihood that many sites, especially the larger, well-resourced consortia, will host and support ReShare products on behalf of their member libraries.

Future Outlook

If Project ReShare is successful (and it does appear to have a lot going for it in that regard), the irony will be that the continued consolidation in the library systems market is largely responsible for its existence.[38] Most notably, OCLC's acquisition of Relais International and the acquisition of RapidILL by Ex Libris, a ProQuest Company. The number and impact of libraries in consortia like PALCI as well as the Big Ten Academic Alliance, the Ivy Plus Libraries, the Triangle Research Libraries Network, and the Greater Western Library Alliance will have on the resource sharing field will be felt by every academic library and noted beyond. Though the type of library is narrow in scope—academic library consortia—when looking at early ReShare adopters, the geographic spread within the United States for ReShare members will be seen as a strength for organizations and individuals hoping to make the move from their existing resource sharing environment to Project ReShare as it develops and gains steam.

SUMMARY

Resource sharing through interlibrary loan and document delivery will continue to be an essential service as libraries begin to reduce their print collection spending and reallocate library spaces originally intended for print collections for other purposes. Libraries becoming partners with each other in various ways to coordinate collection development and streamline sharing will become more and more important, with the end result being more collaborative and balanced resource sharing agreements between large and small groups. This will apply not only to books and other returnables but also to electronic resources. As licensing and copyright compliance become more complicated, especially in regard to electronic resources, libraries will need to use more advanced systems to be able to track use, expenses, and compliance. And as consolidation continues in the overall library systems environment, alternative options that cannot be acquired by large vendors like OSS options will become more and more important to ensuring libraries are able to shape the products they use and not dedicate ever-growing sums of their budget on systems to manage resources rather than resources themselves.

NOTES

1. Founded in 1967, OCLC originally stood for Ohio College Library Center before Online Computer Library Center to finally OCLC, Inc. in 2017.

2. Marshall Breeding, "Resource Sharing in Libraries: Concepts, Products, Technologies, and Trends." *Library Technology Reports*, Chicago, IL: ALA TechSource, 2013, 16, http://search.ebscohost.com/login.aspx?direct=true&db=nlebk&AN=800551&site=ehost-live&scope=site. WorldCat, or WorldCat.org, is considered the largest bibliographic database in the world, with billions of records from their tens of thousands of member libraries.

3. Breeding, "Resource Sharing in Libraries," 16.

4. Increasingly in the digital age, systems are adapting to delivering items electronically not to be returned to the lending library but to expire or become inaccessible after a certain amount of time or number of accesses.

5. With Ex Libris's acquisition of RapidILL, ProQuest's acquisition of Innovative, including the INN-Reach system, and OCLC's acquisition of Relais International, Autographic's SHAREit system is now the main resource sharing system not OSS or owned by OCLC or ProQuest.

6. Breeding, "Resource Sharing in Libraries," 24.

7. Ibid.

8. Ibid.

9. OCLC News releases 2017, "OCLC agrees to acquire Relais International," January 17, 2017, https://cdm15003.contentdm.oclc.org/digital/collection/p15003coll6/id/1374.

10. OCLC News releases 2017, "OCLC introduces Tipasa interlibrary loan management system," January 17, 2017, https://cdm15003.contentdm.oclc.org/digital/collection/p15003coll6/id/1373.

11. Ex Libris, "Ex Libris Acquires RapidILL, Provider of Leading Resource-Sharing Solutions," June 20, 2019, https://www.exlibrisgroup.com/press-release/ex-libris-acquires-rapidill-provider-of-leading-resource-sharing-solutions/.

12. Ibid.

13. Mary E. Jackson, "Staff Cost Savings from Implementing the NISO Circulation Interchange Protocol (NCIP)," *Information Standards Quarterly* 23, no. 4 (Fall 2011): 4–11. https://www.niso.org/niso-io/2011/09/ncip-implementation-savings.

14. "ILL Backends," Accessed August 30, 2020, https://wiki.koha-community.org/wiki/ILL_backends.

15. FulfILLment project, accessed September 5, 2020, http://www.fulfillment-ill.org.

16. OHIONET, "FulfILLment Resource Sharing Project," accessed September 10, 2020, https://www.ohionet.org/products-services/projects-initiatives/fulfillment.

17. FulfILLment Glossary, accessed September 14, 2020, http://www.fulfillment-ill.org/dokuwiki/doku.php?id=laiconnector.

18. This included library services from Kansas, Illinois, Indiana, Iowa, Missouri, Wisconsin, and South Carolina.

19. For more information, the catalog URL is http://finditct.org/eg/opac/home. findIT CT is hosted by Bibliomation, with development and support provided by Equinox.

20. Kristen Wilson and Jill Morris, "Project ReShare: Building a Community-Owned Resource Sharing Platform," *Serials Librarian* 78, no. 1–4 (February 5, 2020): 141–48. doi:10.1080/0361526X.2020.1717323.

21. Ibid., 143.

22. Ibid., 142.

23. Ibid.

24. Project ReShare, "ReShare Returnables – Past Releases," accessed September 11, 2020, https://projectreshare.org/products/returnables/reshare-returnables-past-releases.

25. Ibid.

26. Wilson and Morris, "Project ReShare," 142.

27. Ibid.

28. Ibid., 144; more info on GreenGlass: https://www.oclc.org/en/greenglass.html.

29. University of Chicago Libraries, "The University of Chicago Library Catalog," accessed September 4, 2020, https://catalog.lib.uchicago.edu/vufind.

30. Project ReShare, "ReShare Controlled Digital Lending," accessed September 11, 2020, https://projectreshare.org/produRcts/reshare-controlled-digital-lending/.

31. Project ReShare, "ReShare Controlled Digital Lending."

32. OCLC, "Article Exchange," accessed September 15, 2020, https://www.oclc.org/en/worldshare-ill/features/article-exchange.html.

33. Project ReShare, "ReShare Non-Returnables," accessed September 11, 2020, https://projectreshare.org/products/reshare-non-returnables/.

34. Wilson and Morris, "Project ReShare," 142; PALCI, accessed September 15, 2020, http://www.palci.org/; Ivy Plus Network, accessed September 15, 2020, https://ivyplusnetwork.com/; IndexData, accessed September 15, 2020, https://www.indexdata.com/; Mozilla Foundation, accessed September 15, 2020, https://foundation.mozilla.org/en/; Open Library Foundation (OLF), accessed September 15, 2020, https://openlibraryfoundation.org/; Great Western Library Alliance, accessed September 15, 2020, https://www.gwla.org/; Triangle Research Library Network, accessed September 15, 2020, https://trln.org/; Big 10 Academic Alliance, accessed September 15, 2020, https://www.btaa.org/.

35. Project ReShare, "News Release – ReShare Welcomes Two New Founding Members – Grand Valley State University and Lehigh University," April 22, 2020, https://projectreshare.org/2020/04/22/press-release-reshare-welcomes-two-new-founding-members-grand-valley-state-university-and-lehigh-university/.

36. Wilson and Morris, "Project ReShare," 143.

37. Ibid.

38. Ibid., 141.

7

Open Source Electronic Resource Management

Electronic resources, or e-resources, have reshaped the way libraries work. Starting in the early 2000s, e-resources began to make up more and more of an academic library's overall collections budget. The number of e-resources being purchased and the type of resource it was (e.g., monograph, serial, database, or a set of many such resources) very quickly made managing these collections much more complex and more difficult than managing print resources. This complexity not only applied to workflows and processes used by library personnel or access and licensing requirements that librarians must adhere to, but it also included the systems in use, especially the ILS designed around print resources. Librarians quickly started developing new systems to deal with the many aspects of e-resource management (ERM). Through coordinated efforts among librarians and then libraries and vendors, the first ERM workflows, systems, and standards appeared in the mid-2000s and were relatively mature by the early 2010s. This work would ultimately give rise to the Library Services Platform, or LSP, integrating print and e-resources management into one cohesive system.

HISTORY AND CURRENT STATE

It was recognized very quickly that new tools and workflows would be needed to successfully manage many nontangible electronic resources. E-resource spending quickly made up over half of some libraries' materials budgets as early as 2001 with patron appetites to match.[1] With integrated library systems (ILSs) not designed for these types of resources, libraries quickly started to develop their own systems to manage the onslaught, especially as e-resources increasingly consisted of electronic databases and electronic journals rather than more static, one-time purchase options like electronic books.[2] By 2001, Timothy Jewell, in a 2001 Digital Library Federation (DLF) report, had identified and reported on seven functions of existing e-resource management systems (ERMSs): resources, licensing, acquisition, workflows, systems and technical, organization information, and usage statistics.[3] By 2005, Jewell identified at least twenty libraries on record as having created or in planning stages to create their own homegrown e-resource management systems.[4] Evolving out of the *Web Hub* project Jewell and Adam Chandler established in 2001 was the DLF Electronic Resources Management Initiative, or ERMI.[5] The August 2004 final report of the ERMI made clear the need for commercial development of ERMSs as well as provided a set of requirements these systems would need following many of the identified functions noted above by those libraries able to create their own solutions.[6] Every major commercial vendor answered the call and announced plans for an ERMS of some sort.[7]

In their 2020 text, *Library Information Systems*, Joseph Matthews and Carson Block summarize and categorize the commercial activity into two areas: vendors that added ERM functionality to their ILS, such as III's Millennium system, and vendors that created standalone systems that combined other ERM tools, such as A to Z lists, OpenURL link resolvers, and COUNTER and SUSHI reporting functionality like Serials Solutions.[8] They also note three prominent open source ERMS options: CORAL, initiated by University of Notre Dame Libraries; CUFTS by Simon Fraser University Libraries; and ERMSs by University of Wisconsin–La Crosse Library.[9] Of those three standalone ERMSs, CORAL is the only one still active. It's worth noting that Matthews and Block write that this is because both Simon Fraser and University of Wisconsin–La Cross migrated to LSPs, removing the need for continued development of these systems.[10] ERMSs are not the only results of the activities in the 2000s by the early but cognizant e-resources management community. Matthews and Block note four standards for working with ERM formalized by the National Information Standards Organization (NISO), including some already mentioned in this chapter and previous chapters like OpenURL and KBART.[11] In addition to those are IOTA, an OpenURL quality analytics working group, and PIE-J, a "NISO working group that works to provide standardization and consistent presentation of title changes on provider websites."[12] Rounding out developments in ERM and ERMSs in the 2000s was the announcement of what would be the first viable LSP, OCLC's WorldShare Management Services (WMS), in April 2009, with a viable product becoming available in November 2010.[13]

Though the earliest LSPs have been around for a decade and commercial ERMSs for fifteen years as of this writing, adoption rates of each are still mixed in academic libraries and used considerably less in public libraries. For many, cost is a barrier as well as perceived need, especially for public libraries that still are not dedicating a significant amount of materials budgets to e-content. The open source options covered in the remainder of this chapter may be cost-friendly and timely solutions.

OPEN SOURCE OPTIONS

CORAL

Project: http://coral-erm.org/
Code: https://github.com/coral-erm/
Demo: https://coraldemo.library.tamu.edu/

CORAL has been available as open source since 2010 under a copyleft GPL 3.0 license. Originally developed by University of Notre Dame Libraries (UNDL) with only a licensing module, it has since gained many individual and organizational contributors to the project as well as additional modules and system functionality to effectively compete with commercial options.[14] It uses a LAMP stack architecture.

Background and Current State

CORAL stands for Centralized Online Resources Acquisitions and Licensing, and since 2010, it has had many updates and improvements. As mentioned, the first open source version published by the University of Notre Dame only included the Licensing module. Over the years, other modules have been added, including Resources, Organizations, Usage Statistics, and Management.[15] The functionality of the licensing module and its importance is evident by the ERMI report and early systems focused on ERM covered in the first half of this chapter. However, it should be noted that CORAL's Licensing module includes a terms and ONIX-PL import option.[16] The Usage Statistics module supports manual and automated COUNTER and SUSHI reporting options.[17] The Resources and Management modules focus on specific resources, tasks related to them, workflows, and individuals responsible. The Organizations module stores important information about vendors and publisher contacts and accounts.

There have to date been three major releases of CORAL, and until very recently, they have followed the version 1.x, 2.x, 3.x format. The February 2020 release, 2020.02, introduced a new naming convention using the year and month of the release. Based on the documentation and release notes,

CORAL

Can you share the story of CORAL at your organization?
The firm I work at has over twenty-five offices worldwide. As the Research Services/Library department, we were constantly frazzled trying to manage passwords, IP addresses, contacts, and institutional knowledge around the vast number of electronic resources we pay for. CORAL was the answer to so many of our problems. Not only are we more organized, but our time is also freed up to work on billable research and directly helping attorneys.

How would you describe the CORAL community?
Incredibly receptive. When we were first implementing CORAL, we had a lot of input and ideas. In the next release, several of our suggestions or "wish list" items were included. Many standard library systems cater to academic and public institutions but don't always have an easy way for special libraries to adapt. CORAL is unique in that all types of libraries and information professionals can have a say in the future of the system.

How has CORAL benefitted your organization?
Aside from providing a system for our team to manage all our electronic resources, CORAL has benefitted us by being an incredibly cost-effective solution. The combination of community-based development and the lack of complex contracts to negotiate has made it a solution we not only love but can also boast about.

Keely Ward
Holland & Knight Law Firm
Chicago, Illinois, USA

---

this and the 2020.09 release appear to be incremental releases within version 3.x.[18]

Outside of additional modules added over the years, there have been several efforts to increase integration options with other systems recently. The most publicized of these integrations has been in regard to the open source Koha ILS. As a popular open source ILS with no ERM pieces, integration between the two applications is a natural partnership. As of this writing, the integration (introduced in version 3 major release) includes syncing of vendors between Koha and CORAL's Organization module with development work done by BibLibre and ByWater Solutions.[19] Also of note in the version 3 major release is EBSCO Knowledge Base (KB) Integration. According to the release notes, "this feature allows EBSCO KB customers to search the EBSCO KB from within CORAL and import titles and packages into CORAL," with work done by SirsiDynix.[20]

Community and Service Providers

At the time of this writing, the official CORAL "User Map" page was not available to get a count of CORAL users, but looking at email list activity, past publications, presentations, and looking at the steering committee and web committee detail on the official coral-erm.org webpage, it's clear CORAL has garnered interest and use from over a hundred libraries, including small, medium, and large academic universities spanning the decade it's been available. What's more, it has a healthy number of support providers listed on the coral-erm.org support page, which is a strong indicator that the community size is large enough for multiple companies to provide hosting and support of CORAL.

BibLibre (https://www.biblibre.com/en/): Based in France and founded in 2007, BibLibre is a formalization of consulting and contract development work done by several individuals with a large part of their business and efforts centered around Koha. However, they support and have contributed to many other open source library systems projects, including CORAL. According to a February 2019 blog post on their official website, they have been actively participating in CORAL translation activities to broaden the international appeal of the system.[21]

ByWater Solutions (https://bywatersolutions.com): Featured as a service provider in other chapters of this guide, ByWater offering a support and hosting solution for an ERMS comes as no surprise, especially as their main line of business, Koha, has attracted many academic libraries within the United States in recent years. The recent integration work completed between CORAL and Koha coupled with Aspen Discovery covered in chapter 5 and the now well-established EBSCO EDS integrations ByWater has helped make possible with Koha (and now Aspen) can offer a nearly total library management solution for libraries not ready or able to migrate to an LSP.

SirsiDynix (http://www.sirsidynix.com): A stalwart of the library systems industry, SirsiDynix has wrapped CORAL into their BLUEcloud platform and have called it BLUEcloud eRM.[22] According to a product video on the BLUEcloud eRM page, SirsiDynix developers have made a number of contributions to the CORAL project to improve the overall system and to provide better integration into the BLUEcloud platform.[23] As CORAL is currently under a copyleft open source license, any contributions must be shared, and future releases must adhere to the GPLv3 license. As a result, it appears

BLUEcloud eRM is simply the name of CORAL when hosted by SirsiDynix to fit within the BLUEcloud hosting platform they offer.

Future Outlook

In January 2019, the CORAL steering committee accepted an invitation to join the Open Library Foundation (OLF).[24] The news release published by the steering committee speaks of several benefits:

> Several factors guided our thinking, but our primary vision is to ensure the longevity and viability of CORAL. Joining the OLF gives us greater visibility, and also gives us important benefits to help us continue to grow CORAL's capabilities. Our desire is for CORAL and its user community to continue to thrive and provide value for all types of libraries for many years to come. Furthermore, our project and our engaged user community are seen as tremendous examples for other projects. CORAL's impact is already significant, and will continue to grow as we partner with the OLF.[25]

Time will tell what kind of collaboration opportunities will come from joining the OLF, but other OLF member projects such as GoKb, VuFind, and ReShare have common interests and have much to gain from integration efforts. CORAL will continue to be an appealing option for libraries looking to migrate or adopt an ERMS. As public libraries continue to have a large number of resources dedicated to print management and continue to see high demand for such resources all while acquiring more e-content, CORAL is a viable option for many as an entry into ERM. With the recent integration with Koha, CORAL will also be appealing to Koha libraries, especially small to medium academic libraries with no immediate plans to migrate to an LSP.

FOLIO

> Project: https://www.folio.org/
> Code: https://dev.folio.org/source-code/
> Live Demo: https://wiki.folio.org/ under "Demo Sites" heading for all available options.

The Future of Libraries is Open, or FOLIO, is considered a next-generation ILS commonly referred to as a library services platform, or LSP. The entire FOLIO landscape is covered in detail in chapter 3 of this guide, and as a result, this section will focus on the ERM functionality only. Like any LSP, there are major components of FOLIO dedicated to ERM. In fact, many of the early implementers of FOLIO have gone live with FOLIO's ERM components first with the intention of implementing the traditional ILS components that manage print at a later date. FOLIO is licensed under the permissive Apache 2.0 license and is a multi-tenant platform composed of many microservices rather than more monolithic, static components like those used in LAMP stack architectures.

Background and Current State

As chapter 3 discussed, the original initiator of FOLIO was EBSCO starting in 2015. While EBSCO is a large organization with many proprietary applications, they have a good record of working with open source applications and open source service providers for integration opportunities, CORAL and Koha being notable examples. A large part of EBSCO's business is based around e-content. Until now, an ERMS component has been the only thing missing from their software and services offerings. With EBSCO being the main contributor to the FOLIO project, that gap is, for all intents and purposes, filled. Many of the librarians participating in development have been large academic and research libraries part of the OLE, or Open Library Environment, group. As a result, the FOLIO environment as a whole has been designed with input from some of the largest and most active academic libraries in the world, with ties to leading the conversation around ERM going back to the early 2000s *Web Hub* project.

FOLIO's ERM components are broken down into separate applications as opposed to a general module like CORAL. The purpose of this is to encourage and allow very modular configurations and for each application to focus on a single task and to do it well. This is what is meant by microservice. Currently, an organization using FOLIO just as an ERMS would use four key applications or apps for ERM: Agreements, Licenses, Organizations, and eHoldings. Settings and Users are two other apps where configuration and access, respectively, are controlled. Users is a good example of the microservices nature of the application design in FOLIO. CORAL and other systems, for example, might place this functionality in areas similar to the Settings app in FOLIO instead.

The Agreements app is considered the most central as it ties all information about each e-resource collection together, including Licenses, Organizations, and eHoldings. While it's a looser relationship in FOLIO ERM, in some ways, this is similar to a bibliographic record in a traditional ILS where the order records, holdings records, and item records are often linked or are hierarchically considered subsets to the bibliographic record. The Licenses app contains information about vendors and license terms as well as options for uploading documentation similar to CORAL. Organizations operates similar to the Organizations module in CORAL as well as vendor lists in other ERMSs and ILSs by providing important vendor contact and login details where applicable. Finally, the eHoldings app is most akin to a knowledge base (KB) or collection manager where a user would add, manage, delete electronic packages and databases. With the Agreements app tying all of these particulars together, an organization's e-resource librarian(s) and subject specialists have an easy method to filter, sort, and search across all of the separate components making the ERM components of FOLIO particularly robust.

Interoperability between the eHoldings app and other systems like discovery services and link resolvers is perhaps the most powerful feature of FOLIO ERM functionality as it is in full-fledged LSPs like WMS/WorldCat Discovery and Alma/Primo. EBSCO has been successful at developing API functionality so that EBSCO's Holdings and Links Management, often referred to as HLM with the EBSCOadmin application, is synced with updates and changes in FOLIO eHoldings and vice versa. Until other vendors and open source alternatives are able to develop this type of interoperability with the eHoldings app, EBSCO currently has a significant advantage over competitors whose users want to migrate to FOLIO. It's also important to note, this interoperability, in particular, is what now allows EBSCO to compete more directly with ExLibris and OCLC with their LSPs—Alma and WMS, respectively.

Community and Service Providers

The FOLIO community is young but not small, and it's growing with every software release and news release of more libraries making plans to adopt FOLIO ERM or the full FOLIO suite. There are a number of service providers already, and most have sites live with FOLIO ERM or are in progress.

ByWater Solutions (https://bywatersolutions.com): No stranger to FOSS library systems and with a solid track record of being a good FOSS community member, ByWater Solutions has several contracts in place to provide support and hosting of FOLIO. As much of their current client base is small to medium public and academic libraries, FOLIO should offer ByWater a path to larger academic library partners and, eventually, the larger public library market still dominated by proprietary vendors. Consistently praised for their high customer-service ratings, they should be an appealing option to many of their current client base and other small to medium libraries looking to migrate to FOLIO, especially if those libraries have a smaller technology and systems footprint or if they will benefit from assistance with change management and hands-on training. ByWater should also be a viable option for libraries wanting to benefit from ByWater's implementation and support expertise but want to host their own FOLIO instance.

EBSCO (https://www.ebsco.com/products/ebsco-folio-library-services): Though EBSCO is one of the largest companies in the library market, FOLIO represents a new line of business for EBSCO providing migration, support, hosting, and continual support for FOLIO as well as ensuring its products integrate as well as possible with it. They have a number of contracts already, including University of Alabama, Missouri State University, and the first library in the world to go live (October 2019) with FOLIO, Chalmers University of Technology in Sweden. Their stake in the FOLIO project has dictated the earliest integration options being tied to current EBSCO products like EDS and E-Holdings. For libraries using many EBSCO products already and wanting a fully-hosted, SaaS experience, EBSCO will likely be a top choice. However, unlike the other hosting options, EBSCO may present the biggest risk of vendor lock-in with so many integrations with their product on the table. Because of the potential complexity of these integrations, there is also the risk of a black-box type of environment being created depending on how hands-on or hands-off library staff are with their FOLIO environments when hosted by EBSCO.

IndexData (https://www.indexdata.com/folio/): IndexData also has a few high-profile contracts for FOLIO, including Duke and Lehigh Universities. As the lead architect and developer for the project, many libraries will be interested in contracting IndexData's support and hosting services, which will no doubt be supplemented by IndexData's in-depth knowledge and experience with FOLIO already. However, similar to EBSCO, this will be IndexData's first foray into becoming a service provider of this scope. What IndexData lacks in migration and customer-support experience, they may be able to quickly make up for by being better able to develop tools to assist with the service-provider aspects of the business. For libraries that have their own infrastructure and staff expertise, IndexData might be a natural choice for implementing and support services as well as customized development work. Additionally, for libraries not heavily invested in EBSCO products, IndexData's hosted SaaS solution might provide a solid range of flexibility in meeting a particular organization's needs.

Future Outlook

FOLIO has a promising future, but that future depends heavily on how many libraries and library software vendors and other library services providers become involved in the project. Coupled with traditional ILS integrations, the ERM components are robust. If EBSCO remains the, by far, most active participant in the project's development, non-EBSCO application integration opportunities will become more and more difficult not only from an organizational perspective but also a technical one.

SUMMARY

In a shorter span of time, ERMSs have developed in a similar way to the development of the ILS. It started with large libraries developing their own solutions as the need arose then to a general consensus of what the ERM environment should look like with the ERMI Report. Following that, commercial companies began offering more refined options, CORAL (and others no longer active) appeared in reply as open source alternatives. The merging of e-resources and print with the advent of the LSP is similar to how early ILSs merged with the OPAC and other patron-facing options. And finally, an open source LSP in reply to the early LSP proprietary options. Like the history of library systems, this guide has come full circle with library systems detailed starting in chapter 3. The different systems covered in this chapter will be found appealing by different types of libraries. This could change in time, but it's still hard to say if platform solutions like LSPs or an architecture like FOLIO's will come to dominate over disparate, standalone systems with specialized roles. It is also difficult to say if open source (at least permissively licensed open source) will come to dominate over closed proprietary solutions. For now, both of these worlds are coexisting, collaborating, and adapting to the needs of their users, and that's what matters most.

NOTES

1. Timothy D. Jewell and Anne Mitchell, "Electronic Resource Management," *The Serials Librarian* 48 (2005):1–2, 137–63. doi: 10.1300/J123v48n01_14.
2. Ibid., 138.
3. Ibid., 140.
4. Ibid., 140.
5. Ibid., 144.
6. Ibid., 156.
7. Ibid., 156–57.
8. Joseph R. Matthews and Carson Block, *Library Information Systems* (Westport, Connecticut: Libraries Unlimited, 2020), 100.
9. Ibid.
10. Ibid.

11. "KBART ("Knowledge Bases and Related Tools") is a NISO Recommended Practice that facilitates the transfer of holdings metadata from content providers to knowledge base suppliers and libraries. Knowledge bases are widely used to support library link resolvers and electronic resource management systems," *NISO*, accessed October 18, 2020, https://www.niso.org/standards-committees/kbart.

12. IOTA; PIE-J; Matthews and Block, *Library Information Systems,* 100–1.

13. Marshall Breeding, "Library Services Platforms: A Maturing Genre of Products," *Library Technology Reports*, no. 4 (May 2015): 16. doi:10.5860/ltr.51n4.

14. "About Us," CORAL, accessed October 16, 2020, http://coral-erm.org/about/.

15. "Modules," CORAL, accessed October 16, 2020, http://coral-erm.org/modules/.

16. "ONIX for Publications Licenses (ONIX-PL) is a family of standard XML messaging protocols for exchanging licensing information that builds on the work of the Digital Libraries Federation Electronic Resource Management Initiative (ERMI) and NISO's License Expression Working Group (LEWG)," *NISO*, accessed October 20, 2020, https://www.niso.org/standards-committees/onix-pl-working-group.

17. "COUNTER provides the Code of Practice that enables publishers and vendors to report usage of their electronic resources in a consistent way. This enables libraries to compare data received from different publishers and vendors." "About COUNTER," *Project COUNTER,* accessed October 17, 2020, https://www.projectcounter.org/about; Standardized Usage Statistics Harvesting Initiative (SUSHI) Protocol is an automated request and response model for harvesting e-resource usage data and is designed to work with COUNTER, the most frequently retrieved usage reports, *NISO,* accessed October 17, 2020, https://www.niso.org/standards-committees/sushi.

18. "Release 2020.02," GitHub, accessed October 17, 2020, https://github.com/coral-erm/coral/releases/tag/v2020.02.

19. "Releases," GitHub, accessed October 17, 2020, https://github.com/coral-erm/coral/releases/.

20. Ibid.

21. "Translating CORAL," BibLibre, accessed October 18, 2020, https://www.biblibre.com/en/blog/translating-coral.

22. "BLUEcloud eRM | SirsiDynix," Sirsi Dynix, accessed October 18, 2020, https://www.sirsidynix.com/bluecloud-erm.

23. Ibid.

24. "OLF and CORAL," CORAL, accessed October 16, 2020, http://coral-erm.org/olf-and-coral/.

25. Ibid.

8

Additional Open Source Systems

As the previous chapters have demonstrated, library systems have come a long way from the days when the ILS was the single most important system for libraries. Today, many libraries use and maintain—in addition to the previous systems covered in other chapters—archival management systems, electronic journal publishing platforms, content management systems, and data analytics and visualization tools, just to name a few. Some of these tools are particular to libraries, archives, and museums. Other tools are of general interest to pretty much any organization. All of these categories offer tenable open source solutions for libraries.

ARCHIVAL MANAGEMENT SYSTEMS

The history and development of automation in archives follow a similar timeline to that of libraries. SPINDEX II, an extension of SPINDEX, was a collaborative project between the Library of Congress and the US National Archives. SPINDEX II was developed to automate finding aids to improve the discovery of archival collections. SPINDEX, and SPINDEX II, were created specifically for use by the US National Archives.[1]

With the rise of networked computing in the 1980s and the development of applications like Gopher and the World Wide Web for publishing documents online, archivists began to publish finding aids to the web.[2] It wouldn't be until the late 1990s, however, that the archival profession would make its next leap forward in automation. By then, the Society of American Archivists, in cooperation with the Library of Congress, would publish Encoded Archival

Description (EAD), an encoding standard to bring consistency and interoperability to the structure of machine-readable finding aid metadata.[3]

In the 2000s, educational institutions worked together to develop the first general archival management software applications. Archivists' Toolkit, Archon, and AtoM, made available under open source licenses, were the first archival management applications that were made available and used by archival institutions both great and small. While development and maintenance of Archivists' Toolkit and Archon have discontinued in favor of the adoption of ArchivesSpace, AtoM continues to be actively developed for today.

OPEN SOURCE OPTIONS

Archon

The initial development of Archon began in 2005 as an internal project at the University of Illinois at Urbana-Champaign.[4] Even with the recent advent of EAD, archivists still had several distinct workflows for creating resource discovery tools for archival collections. Whether it was finding aids encoded in HTML, EAD, and MaRC, or print-friendly findings aids in Microsoft Word or PDF format, there were numerous redundant processes involved for creating these essential tools for archival discovery. The initial creators and developers of Archon—Christopher Prom, Scott W. Schwartz, and Christopher A. Rishel—sought, through Archon, to create an archival management system that would allow users to input archival metadata a single time into the system. In turn, the system would output the numerous possible formats so frequently used by archives.[5]

Using internal funding sources from the University of Illinois, the creators of Archon would rework their proof-of-concept software and release version 1.0 in the late summer of 2006.[6] After its initial release, Archon gained wide acceptance among other archival institutions and is still known for its ease of use and maintainability.

In 2009, however, representatives from the University of Illinois agreed to join their efforts with the creators of Archivists' Toolkit to create a new, integrated archival management software.[7] The product of these efforts would eventually come to be known as ArchivesSpace. Consequently, the development of Archon ceased in 2017, with its latest release being version 3.21 release 3.[8] There has not been a new public release of Archon in over three years.

The current state of Archon is especially illustrative of the pitfalls of using open source software for library, archive, and museum technology managers who are new to the open source ecosystem. Archon, for several years, once enjoyed support from a large academic institution and a community of users who either contributed directly or indirectly to its development. As support and resources went to the development of ArchivesSpace, the Archon community was left with a choice to either transition to ArchivesSpace, migrate to some other archival management software, or continue to support software that would no longer enjoy the development attention it had once received. The pressure for Archon users has only increased as time has passed. Archon, like so many of the other open source applications we've considered in this guide, is built using the LAMP stack architecture, with a majority of the source code for Archon being written in PHP.[9] PHP as a language has developed in significant ways in the intervening years. In particular, the major version of PHP Archon was written in is no longer supported by the PHP development community.[10] The PHP development community has made the shift to more current versions, with the most recent major version of PHP being version 7. Since Archon's most recent release is still written primarily in PHP 5, with no plans to update the source code to the most recent major version of PHP, it will become increasingly difficult to support Archon in a production environment. IT departments and cloud infrastructure are no longer making PHP 5 easily available, and any attempt to continue using PHP 5 into the future may present security risks to an organization's IT infrastructure.

That being said, there are still several organizations that continue to use Archon as a legacy archival management system, most notably the University of Illinois at Urbana-Champaign's archives.[11] There is even a service provider, LibraryHost, that provides hosting and support for Archon.[12] The persistence of Archon among archival institutions is a testimony to its value. Archon is lightweight and requires very few resources to run, making it relatively inexpensive for self-hosting. It uses a commonly-used application architecture, so systems administrators and technology managers feel comfortable with managing it. Finally, it is straightforward and simple to configure and use. The use of Archon was and could be a huge leap forward for many small archives with few resources. Any organization considering Archon as a newly adopted archival management system would need to carefully weigh the pros and cons before considering adopting it in the future.

Archivists' Toolkit

At almost the same time as the University of Illinois was in the process of developing Archon, a team of archivists, developers, and other stakeholders from Five College Consortium—including Amherst College, Hampshire College, Mount Holyoke College, Smith College, and the University of

Massachusetts at Amherst—New York University, and the University of California at San Diego were developing their own open source archival management software. Referred to as Archivists' Toolkit, this project had received multi-year funding from the Andrew W. Mellon Foundation.[13] Archivists' Toolkit is a Java-based application used in conjunction with a MySQL database. Archivists' Toolkit is also built with Hibernate, a framework to simplify a Java application's interaction with the relational database. Hibernate also had the added effect that Archivists' Toolkit users could use a different MySQL database if so desired. Archivists' Toolkit was also developed as a desktop application that could operate on Apple OSX, Windows, or Linux operating systems.[14]

While the source code for Archivists' Toolkit is still available via GitHub, as with Archon, it is no longer actively developed. The most recent release of Archivists' Toolkit is from August 2013.[15] While it may still be possible to implement Archivists' Toolkit, it would not be recommended. Like Archon, it is not actively developed or supported, except at legacy sites. Thankfully, as we will see in the final open source options that follow, there are at least two actively maintained archival management software options for any organization seeking to implement its first automated archival software.

ArchivesSpace

The ArchivesSpace archival management system was and is a deliberate attempt to pool the resources of the Archon and Archivists' Toolkit communities. In 2009, representatives from the University of Illinois at Urbana-Champaign, the University of California at San Diego, New York University, and the Andrew W. Mellon Foundation agreed to join the functionality of Archon and Archivists' Toolkit into a single application.[16] While planning and development for ArchivesSpace occurred from 2010 to 2013, development also continued for both Archon and Archivists' Toolkit. In 2013, however, the collaborative efforts on ArchivesSpace paid off when ArchivesSpace version 1.0 was released in 2013.[17] ArchivesSpace is built primarily in Ruby and uses the Ruby on Rails web framework.[18] In the intervening years from 2013 to the present, ArchivesSpace has seen continued support and development, with many archives in the United States adopting ArchivesSpace as their archival management system of choice. In addition to the support from the Andrew W. Mellon Foundation to develop ArchivesSpace in its initial development phase, ArchivesSpace has benefited from large organizations like LYRASIS to sustain and support the development and adoption of ArchivesSpace.[19] As a result, ArchivesSpace has been through numerous releases, with the most current release as of this writing being version 2.8.0.[20]

In addition to the active development being committed to ArchivesSpace, archival organizations have several options for hosting, especially within the United States. Like other open source communities, the ArchivesSpace community features registered service providers who, in addition to offering hosting and support for ArchivesSpace, also actively contribute to the sustainability of ArchivesSpace. The three documented registered service providers are LYRASIS, Atlas Systems, Inc., and Keystone Library Network.[21] While there is a price tag associated with being a registered service provider for ArchivesSpace, these providers enjoy exclusive access to documentation and communications platforms used by the ArchivesSpace user community. It is worth noting, however, that there are other non-registered service providers for ArchivesSpace both within the United States and without. Examples of providers in this category are LibraryHost—in the United States—and Cultural Hosting—based out of Spain. A simple web search reveals these hosts, although there may be other available providers.

It is also possible for an organization to self-host ArchivesSpace, using either a private or public cloud service. ArchivesSpace is relatively easy to set up and configure, and there is some documentation publicly available on the Internet for systems administrators to consult for setup and management. However, in order to gain access to the ArchivesSpace listserv and other helpful documentation, organizations are required to become members of the user group community.[22] This access may come with a hefty price tag, depending on the size of your organization.[23] Organizations will have to weigh whether the benefit of being a member is worth the expense. Of course, if an organization decides to choose a registered service provider with ArchivesSpace, the service provider and, indirectly, the organization will both enjoy these benefits.

AtoM

Access to Memory (hereafter referred to as AtoM) is the oldest of the four archival management systems considered still currently developed and maintained today. Dating its inception to 2007, AtoM is a web-based archival management system using the familiar LAMP architecture.[24] Like Archon, it is written in PHP, although it is currently updated to operate with the current version of PHP, version 7.[25] In addition to the web server and relational database components, AtoM also requires Java, since it uses Elasticsearch for indexing.[26] The most recent version, as of this writing, is 2.6.0 and was released in July 2020.[27] AtoM has been well-received internationally, even going so far as to receive funding and support from UNESCO and the International Council on Archives.[28]

AtoM enjoys the commitment and stability of Artefactual as the lead developer of the AtoM software. In addition to providing supporting documentation and hosting the source code for AtoM, Artefactual also offers hosting, support, and migration assistance, among other things.[29] There is no cost associated with accessing the documentation or seeking assistance from the user community. For the institution considering a hosted solution for AtoM, there are several other hosting providers available. For example, some of the same hosting providers of ArchivesSpace also host and support AtoM. Self-hosting is also an option with AtoM. Because of its familiar architecture and easily accessible community and documentation, the adoption of AtoM should be relatively simple for an organization with the necessary in-house technical expertise.

Just as we've seen with digital repositories, open source options have dominated the archival management system landscape in the past two decades. While there are sites still using Archon and Archivists' Toolkit, these applications may not be the best option for small organizations seeking to implement their first archival management software. ArchivesSpace and AtoM both represent good options because they are still currently developed, have institutional support, and enjoy a sizable user community. Aside from choosing which platform an organization is going to use is the decision of whether to self-host, either in the cloud or on-premises, or to pay a hosting provider. Both of these platforms have multiple options for service providers so organizations can avoid vendor lock-in. Determining which platform and hosting option to go with will be the two most significant decisions an organization will need to address when considering these systems.

ADDITIONAL OPEN SOURCE PLATFORMS

In addition to archival management software, libraries and other cultural heritage institutions find it necessary to maintain other supplemental software to perform day-to-day responsibilities. These responsibilities may include managing web content to assist users with research, managing the publication of peer-reviewed journals, or tracking the use of library space. Each of these responsibilities can be managed with mature open source options.

SubjectsPlus

Maintaining a virtual presence has become vital to the success of cultural heritage institutions such as libraries, archives, and museums. For most people, the website is the go-to place—sometimes the only place—for accessing services or seeking information about a particular institution. While some personnel may already be familiar with widely popular open source content management systems like Drupal and WordPress, there are other potential open source tools out there that have been catering to the day-to-day management of a cultural heritage institution's web presence.

SubjectsPlus is a LAMP-based application written primarily in PHP and is used as a web publishing platform for library-specific tasks.[30] For example, SubjectsPlus makes it easy for libraries to publish a list of available full-text databases or indexes, a personnel list, a video library, and research guides, among other processes. SubjectsPlus was originally developed by the Joyner Library at East Carolina University. Since its inception, other organizations have taken over as lead maintainers and developers of SubjectsPlus, the most current of which is the University of Miami.[31] SubjectsPlus is utilized by libraries, both large and small, across the world. In the United States, smaller institutions like Lancaster Theological Seminary and larger institutions like Louisiana State University use SubjectsPlus.[32]

As of this writing, there are no known hosting and support providers for SubjectsPlus. Any organization considering implementing SubjectsPlus will need to self-host, either on-premises or in the cloud. Because SubjectsPlus uses the familiar LAMP architecture, is compatible with the most current version of PHP, is maintained by a larger institution, and enjoys a relatively healthy user community, SubjectsPlus could be a relatively cost-effective option for libraries who are looking for an alternative to the familiar LibGuides product by Springshare.

Open Journal Systems

Open Journal Systems (hereafter referred to as OJS) is the flagship software of the Public Knowledge Project and was first released in 2001.[33] The Public Knowledge Project and the Simon Fraser University Library are the two key players in the development of OJS. As its name implies, OJS is an open source journal publication platform complete with workflows to support the peer-review process. To date, there are over 10,000 journals published using OJS.[34]

OJS uses a LAMP architecture and is written primarily in PHP. While the L in LAMP may stand for the Linux operating system, OJS is can also be installed on BSD, Solaris, Mac OSX, and Windows.[35] The OJS ecosystem is highly active and has received significant financial and developmental support from organizations worldwide.[36] There are over 140 contributors to the codebase for OJS listed on its GitHub page.[37]

As a result of its popularity, PKP Publishing Services was created to offer hosting and support solutions. With multi-tier plans to support small institutions publishing a single journal to a full-blown enterprise tier for large organizations, PKP Publishing Services is capable of hosting to meet most organizations' needs. As of this writing, a basic hosting plan for a single title is $850 annually.[38] Another hosting option for OJS is openjournalsystems.com. With basic hosting packages starting at $460 annually on a per-title basis, openjournalsystems.com is worthy of consideration as well.[39] Of course, an organization looking to implement a publishing platform could always self-host OJS on-premises or in the cloud. As with so many other software we've considered throughout this guide, this project especially enjoys a healthy, active development community and user group. Any assistance or guidance with bugs or configuration issues have as much hope, if not more so, of going answered when compared to similar proprietary software options. As libraries, especially academic libraries, begin to take on more of an active role in advocating open access to information in electronic publishing, software like Open Journal Systems will become a tempting option for more cultural heritage institutions.

Suma

Over the past two decades, more and more libraries are attempting to minimize the footprint consumed by the library stacks and making more room for the library community to use its space, whether it is being used to study for exams, create content, or engage in casual conversation with others. Additionally, as budgets seem to continue to shrink or grow stagnant, it is all the more important that libraries have a simple, effective way to quantify the assistance rendered by library staff at various points of service. As a result, many library administrators are making better efforts, with the assistance of new technologies, to more accurately gauge exactly how library space is used and what services are requested in order to better meet the needs of its stakeholders. At North Carolina State University, its in-house developers created Suma and have made it freely available as open source software, allowing other libraries to benefit from its development.[40] Among the various metrics Suma is made to measure and store are building occupancy by headcount, usage by space, roaming reference transactions, and traditional interactions at fixed service points.[41]

Created to work with mobile devices like tablets, Suma is built using the LAMP-based architecture and, while some of the codebase is written in PHP, a majority of the source code is written using JavaScript and depends on the

Zend framework.[42] All of these technologies should be relatively familiar to most systems librarians and systems administrators.

There are no known service providers for Suma at the time of this writing. There are, however, over one hundred libraries currently using Suma, so it enjoys institutional support in its parent institution, North Carolina State University, and a significant user community.[43] Because of its familiar architecture, any organization wishing to implement Suma by self-hosting should have few difficulties with a basic setup.

EVER-EXPANDING OFFERINGS

The software ecosystem among cultural heritage institutions today is a much more complex place than it was even two decades ago. In addition to the integrated library system with its traditional cataloging, acquisitions, and circulation modules, there are now library service platforms, systems for managing electronic resource, interlibrary loan systems, discovery layers, digital repositories, archival management systems, publishing platforms, and statistics tools, just to name a few. These categories only represent some of the many tools geared specifically toward libraries, archives, and museums. Many of today's cultural heritage institutions make use of data analytics and visualization tools, research data management systems, and content management systems, all of which are of general interest to most organizations, regardless of their type. All of these categories have open source options adopted and used by all sorts of organizations. This chapter has explored several of the non-traditional open source software applications cultural heritage institutions make use of today. At this point, the reader should be aware of the available open source options in the library software ecosystem. As this and the previous chapter show, there is almost no area of the library software ecosystem untouched by open source initiatives, and many of these OSS options are as healthy as traditional proprietary options.

NOTES

1. Rob Weiner, "Archives and Automation: Issues and Trends," *Information Analyses* (May 1995): 9, https://eric.ed.gov/?id=ED384352; "Spindex," *Dictionary of Archives Terminology*, s.v. "Spindex," accessed September 30, 2020, https://dictionary.archivists.org/entry/spindex.html.

2. Bradley D. Westbrook, Lee Mandell, Kelcy Shepherd, Brian Stephens, and Jason Verghese, "The Archivists' Toolkit: Another Step Toward Streamlined

Archival Processing," *Journal of Archival Organization* 4 (2007): 231, https://doi.org/10.1300/J201v04n01_12.

3. Daniel V. Pitti, "Encoded Archival Description: An Introduction and Overview," *D-Lib Magazine* 5, no. 11 (November 1999), http://www.dlib.org/dlib/november99/11pitti.html.

4. Christopher Prom and Scott Schwartz, "ICR 'Seed Money' Grant: Final Report," http://archon.org/FinalReport.pdf.

5. Christopher J. Prom, Scott W. Schwartz, Christopher A. Rishel, and Kyle J. Fox, "A Unified Platform for Archival Description and Access," *Proceedings of the 7th ACM/IEEE-CS Joint Conference on Digital Libraries* (June 2007), 160, https://doi.org/10.1145/1255175.1255205.

6. Ibid.

7. "History," ArchivesSpace, accessed October 2, 2020, https://archivesspace.org/about/history.

8. "Archonproject/archon," GitHub, accessed on October 2, 2020, https://github.com/archonproject/archon.

9. Ibid.

10. "Unsupported Branches," PHP.net, accessed October 5, 2020, https://www.php.net/eol.php.

11. You can still view and search the University of Illinois's implementation of Archon by going to https://github.com/archonproject/archon/releases/tag/v3.21.3.

12. "The Software We Host," LibraryHost.com, accessed October 5, 2020, https://libraryhost.com.

13. Bradley D. Westbrook, Lee Mandell, Kelcy Shepherd, Brian Stephens, and Jason Verghese, "The Archivists' Toolkit: Another Step Toward Streamlined Archival Processing," 233.

14. Ibid., 240–43.

15. "Ucsdlib/AT," GitHub.com, accessed on October 5, 2020, https://github.com/ucsdlib/AT.

16. "History," ArchivesSpace.

17. Ibid.

18. "Archivesspace/archivesspace," GitHub.com, accessed on October 5, 2020, https://github.com/archivesspace/archivesspace.

19. "History," ArchivesSpace.

20. "Archivesspace/archivesspace," GitHub.com.

21. "Current Registered Service Providers," ArchivesSpace, accessed on October 5, 2020, https://archivesspace.org/registered-service-providers/current-rsps.

22. "Member Benefits," ArchivesSpace, accessed on October 5, 2020, https://archivesspace.org/community/member-benefits.

23. "Types and Levels of Membership," ArchivesSpace, accessed October 5, 2020, https://archivesspace.org/community/types-of-membership.

24. "Home," Accesstomemory.org, accessed on October 5, 2020, https://www.accesstomemory.org/en/.

25. "Artefactual/atom," GitHub.com, accessed on October 5, 2020, https://github.com/artefactual/atom; "Technical Requirements," Artefactual, accessed on

October 5, 2020, https://www.accesstomemory.org/en/docs/2.6/admin-manual/installation/requirements/#installation-requirements.

26. Ibid.

27. "Downloads," Artefactual, accessed on October 5, 2020, https://www.accesstomemory.org/en/download/.

28. "ICA Statement on Access to Memory," International Council on Archives, accessed on October 5, 2020, https://www.ica.org/en/ica-statement-access-memory-atom-0.

29. "Home," Artefactual, accessed on October 5, 2020, https://www.artefactual.com.

30. "Subjectsplus/SubjectsPlus," GitHub.com, accessed on October 5, 2020, https://github.com/subjectsplus/SubjectsPlus.

31. "Home," SubjectsPlus, accessed on October 5, 20200, https://www.subjectsplus.com.

32. "Sites Using SubjectsPlus," SubjectsPlus Wiki, accessed on October 5, 2020, http://subjectsplus.com/wiki3/?title=Sites_using_SubjectsPlus.

33. James MacGregor, Kevin Stranack, and John Willinsky, "The Public Knowledge Project: Open Source Tools for Open Access to Scholarly Communication," in *Opening Science*, ed. Sönke Bartling and Sascha Friesike (New York: Springer Open, 2014), 166, https://doi.org/10.1007/978-3-319-00026-8_11.

34. "Open Journal Systems," Public Knowledge Project, accessed on October 5, 2020, https://pkp.sfu.ca/ojs/.

35. "Install," GitHub.com, accessed on October 5, 2020, https://github.com/pkp/ojs/tree/master/docs.

36. "Sustainers," Public Knowledge Project, accessed on October 5, 2020, https://pkp.sfu.ca/sustainers/.

37. "Pkp/ojs," GitHub.com, accessed on October 5, 2020, https://github.com/pkp/ojs.

38. "Pricing," PKP Publishing Services, accessed on October 5, 2020, https://pkpservices.sfu.ca/ojs-hosting-plans-prices/.

39. "OJS Hosting," Openjournalsystems.com, accessed on October 5, 2020, https://openjournalsystems.com/ojs-hosting/. It should be noted that while PKP Publishing Services and openjournalsystems.com both have "basic" hosting packages, their packages vary in terms of their disk space allocation, bandwidth allocation, and so on. Both "basic" packages would need to be considered closely as there is no one-to-one correlation between the services offered by these two providers.

40. While the original development team consisted of Jason Casden—the project lead—Joyce Chapman, Eric McEachern, Rusty Earl, Rob Rucker, and Hill Taylor, it has most recently been under the oversight of the Digital Library Initiatives Unit at NCSU. With the recent passing of Bret Davidson, the former leader of the Digital Library Initiatives unit, the future of Suma is uncertain, although NCSU has appointed an interim associate head of DLI.

41. "Suma," North Carolina State University Libraries, accessed on October 5, 2020, https://www.lib.ncsu.edu/projects/suma.

42. "Installation," Suma Project, accessed on October 5, 2020, https://suma-project.github.io/Suma/installation/.

43. "Suma," North Carolina State University.

9

Libraries, Open Source Software, and the Future

LIBRARY SERVICES YESTERDAY, TODAY, AND TOMORROW

Libraries and their automated systems have experienced several technological shifts over the past five decades. Initially, the focus of library automation was to improve the circulating of physical books. Today, library systems—even of a relatively small library—are often responsible for the management of print books, electronic books, journals, archives, exhibits, research data, and other information artifacts. There can be no doubt that library services and the technology upon which these services depend have continued to expand over previous decades. With these waves of social change, technological advancements have made it easier for library technology managers to cope with these shifting tides. Virtualization technology, cloud infrastructure, and improved network infrastructure are just a few of the developments that have made it possible for libraries to respond to the changing behavior and expectations of information-seekers.

Open source software (OSS), too, has played a significant role in enabling libraries to meet the current and future expectations of their communities. As the history of many of the OSS applications from previous chapters demonstrates, open source software has enabled more libraries to either become active developers of their own technologies or, at the very least, more active partners in the development of the very technologies they use. Many of these software applications are the result of grassroots or grant-funded research development to meet the practical everyday needs of libraries. Either proprietary automation vendors were slow to respond to the needs of cultural heritage institutions, or there was little perceived value in developing these technologies.

The OSS movement, however, has itself changed over the decades. While many open source projects of the past consisted of small-scale development to meet the needs of single institutions or to entertain hobbyist developers outside of work and study, many giants in the IT industry today have embraced the open source development and licensing model. Companies such as Microsoft and IBM, once either skeptical or subversive of OSS, now invest heavily in open source software. OSS, once a grassroots revolution, has permeated the IT landscape.

Within the library software ecosystem, FOLIO is an exemplar of the new era of open source development. Libraries from larger institutions, primarily represented by ARL universities, EBSCO, and IndexData, have undertaken and at least initially succeeded in the largest library open source project to date. Increasingly, library stakeholders are viewing open source development as an effective tool to counter the consolidation of the ILS/LSP market by a handful of vendors. More library administrators see OSS as a potential long-term solution to avoid vendor lock-in and overpriced software that no longer meets the needs of the twenty-first-century library. OSS may even, it is hoped, free up budgetary space for libraries who see resource prices continue to rise annually without budget increases to keep up with the expenses.

LIBRARY SERVICES AND GLOBAL CRISES

"Unprecedented" is a term that has been used ad nauseum over the past year, yet it is one of the few words that accurately describe the current state of affairs for humanity in general and for libraries in particular. For lack of a more apt description, these are indeed unprecedented times. As we write these words, the COVID-19 pandemic has infected over fifty-seven million people worldwide, with the United States accounting for almost twelve million of these cases. Over 1.3 million have died from this virus worldwide.[1] While there are brief periods of improvement overall, these periods have been followed by increased cases. Meanwhile, governments at all levels are locked in a struggle to keep the public safe and prevent the world (including its economy) from coming to a standstill. Libraries are no exception.

Few libraries were prepared to close their doors for a protracted period at the beginning of the COVID-19 pandemic. Many libraries are having to learn how to offer services remotely for the first time. Others have sought a hybrid approach where the library's community can still use physical materials or enjoy in-person library services while offering expanded virtual services. This pandemic has brought out the creative and adaptive side of many libraries.

In addition to adapting, however, library administrators and personnel have also been left with the all-too-familiar process of selecting essential services in the face of budget cuts that often accompany an economic slowdown in global crises. The Southern Adirondack Library System (SALS) in New York, for example, was faced with a 20 percent budget decrease as a result of the pandemic. What was the first category they took off the table? Their ILS and IT support.[2] SALS is just one example of a library that views its technological infrastructure as integral in meeting their goals.

How does OSS factor into the conversation of libraries facing a budgetary crisis, though? OSS has the potential to provide libraries with greater flexibility when hard times hit. There are at least two reasons for taking this observation seriously. In the first place, contrary to the proprietary option, libraries who use OSS have the additional options to switch service providers or to self-host while reducing the pain of a transition to a completely new system. This observation would hold true for both small and large libraries. Even the option to self-host, while intimidating to some smaller libraries, is possible, especially as the requisite knowledge required to self-host should fit comfortably within the wheelhouse of most technology managers and systems administrators. Second, the OSS ecosystem is drastically different from what it was even a decade ago. For the OSS communities that have been around for the past decade, the software has matured significantly. For newer OSS projects, development techniques like microservices, DevOps, Agile, and other practices have dramatically improved the software development process and the quality of software over the years. Additionally, virtualization technologies and cloud services have made implementing OSS cheaper and easier to implement than ever before. While all of these points would hold true for proprietary software as well, they also demonstrate that these developments make OSS more accessible to a greater number of libraries than at any other time.

ONE LAST TIME

While the authors have attempted to address potential reservations library personnel might have toward OSS in previous chapters—especially chapter 2—a summary case bears repeating in this concluding chapter. Even though OSS has come a long way and has continued to gain acceptance over the years, its future is by no means certain, even within libraries. Software licensing has become more complex, and other licensing models that are neither fully open source nor proprietary are emerging.[3] OSS may have a definite future, but the question of its extent and continued influence is still unknown.

As this guide hopefully demonstrates, the objection to OSS based on the concern that it requires a software developer or knowledge not possessed by in-house staff is a misunderstanding based on assumptions that would have held years ago but are mostly inaccurate today. Most medium or large organizations have personnel who specialize in systems, and library OSS requires no more knowledge of systems than what most systems administrators already possess through education and experience. It is also important to note that systems administrators are not developers. A developer, while helpful in extending the functionality of an open source application, isn't necessary to implement most OSS applications as-is. For smaller libraries or even libraries without personnel with systems experience, there are service providers who manage hosting and support. Thus, libraries do not need in-house technical expertise to implement OSS.

Some library technology experts view those who prefer library OSS as being led by an idealism that could prove harmful to libraries. Rather than choosing what is best to meet a library's needs, those who prefer open source library software may preclude the option for proprietary software that is better suited to a particular library. This concern is a legitimate one. There may be the tendency for some to view proprietary software as inherently a bad choice. It is important here to note an important distinction. Arguments against proprietary software are not arguments against private industry. Instead, they are arguments against what is seen as the best methodology around which software companies might create genuinely valuable tools for clients. As we saw in chapter 1, companies such as IBM and Microsoft have adapted and demonstrated that software companies need not depend on proprietary software to remain solvent. If anything, these companies have demonstrated that embracing OSS has led to greater innovation within their companies. So, while proprietary software isn't bad per se, the tide of software development is shifting as private industry has found ways to capitalize on open source software. As a final note on this argument, the needs of a particular library have both short-term and long-term consequences. A library may adopt an OSS solution that doesn't serve them well in the short term but, in subsequent years, works overwhelmingly in favor of the library. By choosing an OSS solution that doesn't have all of the desired features, for example, a library may prevent being locked into a multi-year contract with a vendor where prices become unmanageable during an economic downturn. As another example, a library may choose proprietary software from a library vendor that works well as a technical solution initially. After several years with this vendor, a competing vendor may buy them out, introducing uncertainty of the future for the product. How will this acquisition change the product? The point of these examples is not to argue that proprietary software is always wrong. What it is meant to show, however, is that the people who make decisions for libraries must consider not only the current needs of their library but also the long-term risks associated with a particular choice. As the examples laid out here demonstrate, OSS helps to avoid at least some long-term risks associated with traditional proprietary software in libraries. In sum, OSS advocates have legitimate reasons for preferring open source options over proprietary ones, and these reasons aren't purely idealistic.

The authors wrote this guide with two purposes in mind. First is the immediate purpose. This guide has attempted to gather in one place information on a variety of OSS used by libraries worldwide. This information is meant to serve as an introduction to the software and the communities that create and foster them. The second purpose of this guide, too, has been to provide an updated treatment of library OSS that has been sorely needed. The library OSS ecosystem, like OSS in general, is constantly changing. Observations about OSS from even ten years ago may no longer be true. The authors believe that OSS in libraries has gained steam, and the arguments for considering OSS alongside proprietary software are as strong as ever. If the reader is convinced to give library OSS a fair hearing alongside more traditional options without dismissing it out of hand, then this guide will have achieved its goal.

NOTES

1. E. Dong, H. Du, and L. Gardner. "An Interactive Web-based Dashboard to Track COVID-19 in Real Time," *The Lancet Infectious Diseases* 20, no. 5 (February 19, 2020): 533–34. doi: 10.1016/S1473-3099(20)30120-1.

2. Lisa Peet, "Budgeting for the New Normal: Libraries Respond to COVID-19 Funding Constraints," *Library Journal,* September 24, 2020, https://www.libraryjournal.com/?detailStory=budgeting-for-the-new-normal-libraries-respond-to-covid-19-funding-constraints.

3. Justin Colannino, "What's Up with These New Not-Open Source Licenses?," *The GitHub Blog,* March 18, 2021, https://github.blog/2021-03-18-whats-up-with-these-new-not-open-source-licenses/.

Appendix A

Notes on Library System Implementations

A system implementation is the process of installing and configuring a new system to provide a new service or replace an existing system and its services. The details of an implementation rely heavily on an organization's need, the system itself, whether a vendor has been contracted to assist or carry out implementation, and whether the system is replacing a current system in use by the organization.

If the new system is a replacement, then the project is often referred to as a migration. These projects typically involve a large amount of data transfer and data manipulation between the old and new system as well as training and change management highlighting not only the new system's functionality but often how workflows and use of the system will be different than the current system. Generally, migration projects require a higher amount of coordination, technical expertise, project management, and leadership skills for success compared to implementing a new system.

Because of the complexity and nuances involved, this guide has not attempted to provide detailed information on systems implementations. Most of the time, an implementation for a proprietary system and an OSS library system will differ little, and there are several texts that cover this subject (see suggested readings at the end of this appendix). For larger organizations, the knowledge and skills needed are increasingly already available, contracted directly, or procured through a vendor- or service-level provider for such services. For small- and medium-sized organizations (and increasingly large-sized organizations), the service-level providers noted in this guide will often be able to provide all the expertise needed as part of their services and contract with each organization. Because services are often continued with the same provider, like support and hosting, it's in the provider's best interest to ensure a successful implementation and training phase, since when that process is done well, it often mitigates support issues and increases the likelihood of an organization renewing service contracts.

Systems migrations and implementations are often organized and carried out using project management (PM) methodologies, especially for larger, months-long implementations. PM has been prominent in software development for decades, and a number of PM methodologies have appeared and evolved to meet the specific needs of software development, especially as improvements in computing and connectivity have changed delivery and distribution requirements and how quickly a product must be made available to end users.

Library systems, open and proprietary, are no exception to these changes. Implementation teams often rely on a combination of software development methods, like Agile or Scrum PM methods and tools, as well as tools and methods born out of more traditional PM, like Waterfall, depending on a project's length and nature. In many ways, a large implementation project is similar to a construction project where something is being installed and configured over a period of many months. However, as software development has moved to a web-based model, an iterative approach to development has taken over with relatively short release cycles called sprints, often measured in weeks. Because of this, the system at the beginning of a project will often be slightly different than when the site goes live with it. This requires project managers (often called implementation managers, lead or similar) to be aware of changes being made to the software while it is being installed and be able to understand quickly and communicate effectively how those changes will impact an organization implementing the system. Project managers will also often have the added responsibility of championing features or fixes for a site that needs certain functionality in place before their implementation is complete.

Regardless of the project or specific system, all migration and implementations live and die by organization, communication, and change management. In fact, a project manager's main task is creating a framework around these activities for the project team and other stakeholders to work within. That means clearly defining the scope of the project, clearly defining the project's timeline and activities, creating a clear communications plan, and creating a plan for change management or clearly defining how stakeholders work will change with the new system so that no stakeholder is surprised or feels unprepared for the change to come.

SUGGESTED READINGS

A Guide to the Project Management Body of Knowledge (PMBOK Guide) / Project Management Institute: Project Management Institute. Sixth edition. (Newtown Square, PA: Project Management Institute, 2017).

Joseph R Matthews and Carson Block, "Chapter 12: System Migration and Implementation" in *Library Information Systems,* Second edition (Santa Barbara, CA: Libraries Unlimited, 2020), 189–201.

Kyle Banerjee, Bonnie Parks, and Siôn Romaine, *Migrating Library Data: A Practical Manual / Edited By Kyle Banerjee and Bonnie Parks* (Chicago: Neal-Schuman, an imprint of the American Library Association, 2017).

Marshall Breeding, "The Systems Librarian: Migration: Opportunities Revamp Automation Strategies," *Computers in Libraries* 38, no. 2 (March 2018): 17–18, 20.

Appendix B
ILS Selection & Migration Example

Note: This is a high-level system selection and migration project plan used for a medium-sized academic library in 2017 and 2018. Names of organizations, systems, and individuals have been changed.

ILS MIGRATION FROM ALPHA ILS TO OMEGA ILS

Executive Summary

Since the implementation of the Alpha Integrated Library System (ILS) in 1999 at SU Library, there have been many advancements in library information management systems. Cloud computing and Software as a Service (SaaS) technologies, coupled with the move to electronically-based library resources, have left SU's eighteen-year-old system lacking essential features for successful management of today's academic library and its resources. Specifically, Alpha ILS lacks support for managing e-resources, which is the largest growth area of our collection and will continue to be for years to come. Additionally, Alpha ILS lacks a web-based user interface requiring maintenance and support of Windows-based clients, which unnecessarily add to overall time, cost, and dependence on the Windows operating system. Lastly, the cost of support for Alpha ILS has become prohibitive and is comparable to the cost of full hosting and support with other ILS providers. Through identifying web-based ILS/Library Service Platform (LSP) providers, reviewing, inviting each provider to demonstrate their products to library staff, and getting feedback from library staff, we believe the open source ILS,

Omega ILS, hosted and supported by Omega ILS Company, meets our needs while staying within our budget constraints.

Review, Demo, and Selection Process

SU Library's intention to migrate to an ILS more suited to its needs has been clear since its search for the recently filled Emerging Technologies and Systems Librarian vacancy. The job description included having knowledge and experience with web- or cloud-based library systems. The new Emerging Technologies and Systems Librarian began their search and review of library systems to replace Alpha ILS in June of 2016. The constraints were: 1) the system must be web-based; 2) the system must have an avenue for e-resource management; 3) the system must allow for moderate level of customization to meet SU's workflow needs; and 4) the cost of the system must be sustainable.

Meeting the majority of those constraints, three systems were identified: Beta ILS, Zeta ILS, and Omega ILS.

Beta ILS

Beta ILS is considered by many in the field to be the premier library system for medium to large academic libraries for functionality, managing e-resources, and company loyalty. It is a multi-tenant SaaS LSP, and in many ways, it reflects the future of library systems by mimicking other industry system ERPs, or enterprise resource planning systems. Beta ILS is from the same company that provides Alpha ILS support to SU Library currently. Many libraries that migrate from Alpha ILS have migrated to Beta ILS. While the system costs more than Alpha ILS, it is more capable, and since the vendor is the same company, migration would be a simpler process for the vendor and for the library.

The demonstration was well-received, and the system appears very robust. While we believe the system is very capable of meeting our web-based and e-resource management needs as well as our future reporting and analytics needs, the high cost and sub-par customer support from the vendor for our Alpha ILS system are two issues we cannot ignore.

Beta ILS Survey Results
The survey was a series of questions about each functioning area of the systems demoed and a Likert scale with five choices: Excellent, Good, Average, Poor, and Not Sure. Survey results that follow are the highest percentages of each response. Where the highest response was "Not Sure," the second-highest was included.

Comments that were specific questions regarding functionality or statements about the survey or quality of demos were omitted.

Beta ILS

50% of respondents rated Print Management as Good.
50% of respondents rated E-Resource Management as Good.
50% of respondents rated Discovery as Average.
63% of respondents rated Patron Management as Good.
50% of respondents rated Staff Task Management as Average.
50% of respondents rated Metadata Management as Average.
38% of respondents rated Acquisitions Management as Average.
50% of respondents rated Reporting as Excellent.
50% of respondents rated Customer Support as Average.

Comments

"From my own recollections it seemed to be quite a robust system, particularly the back end for dealing with patron records and things of that nature. Wasn't it quite pricey though?"

"Great product. Too expensive. Moving on."

Zeta ILS

Zeta ILS is a multi-tenant library services platform offered by Zeta Company. Zeta Company has traditionally specialized in databases, metadata of bibliographic records, and resource sharing. Zeta ILS is now in its fifth year and is well-represented by small to medium academic libraries. While cost is closer to our needs and it is a web-based system, we believe the lack of customization available for our workflows, our bibliographic records needs, and for integration of the State Share Catalog proved too much change for the library to take on. As is reflected by the survey that follows, the demo appeared for many to lack content and product specifics. Many of the questions we had were not adequately answered.

The survey was a series of questions about each functioning area of the systems demoed and a Likert scale with five choices: Excellent, Good, Average, Poor, and Not Sure. Survey results are the highest percentages of each response. Where the highest response was "Not Sure," the second-highest was included.

Zeta ILS Survey Results

Comments that were specific questions regarding functionality or statements about the survey or quality of demos were omitted.

62% of respondents were Not Sure of Print Management capabilities.
75% of respondents were Not Sure of E-Resource Management capabilities.
50% of respondents rated Discovery as Average.
75% of respondents were Not Sure of Patron Management capabilities.
75% of respondents were Not Sure of Staff Task Management capabilities.
63% of respondents were Not Sure of Metadata Management capabilities.
75% of respondents were Not Sure of Acquisitions Management capabilities.
75% of respondents were Not Sure of Reporting/Analytics Management capabilities.
50% of respondents were Not Sure of Customer Support capabilities.

Comments

"I don't remember many of the above details about this webinar. They didn't really seem to have or do anything to stand out."

Omega ILS

The Omega ILS was developed several years ago as an open source library system. It has had a large user and software development community for many years and continues to add new features to compete with proprietary systems by other providers. While the source code for the system is openly available, many companies across the globe now specialize in providing hosting and support of Omega ILS. Omega ILS Company is the largest provider of these services and is often recognized for its strong customer support.

Though Omega ILS is a web-based system, it is not multi-tenant. This means that our instance would have a dedicated server of its own, and upgrades to the system would be done differently than a true cloud service. On the plus side, this might allow for more customization than some multi-tenant solutions. The maintenance and attention given to our server also have the advantage of providing a better, more-personal relationship with the hosting and support provider, Omega ILS Company. Through the demonstration to staff and systems librarian's research, Omega ILS appears to be a natural transition from our current system, with many of the same or similar features but updated and more user-friendly. The available APIs and customizations will allow many of our current workflows to continue to exist as well as allow us to integrate with other systems, including the State Share Catalog.

Omega ILS, with support by Omega ILS Company, meets all of our constraints, and with its active developer network and global user community of which SU Library will become a member, we believe it will continue to evolve to meet our changing needs. As a bonus, the use of this open source system will allow SU Library to set an example on the SU campus and within the region in good financial stewardship as well as an example of choosing an open over a closed, often costly, service.

Omega ILS Survey Results

The survey was a series of questions about each functioning area of the systems demoed and a Likert scale with five choices: Excellent, Good, Average, Poor, and Not Sure. Survey results below are the highest percentages of each response. Where the highest response was "Not Sure," the second-highest was included.

Comments that were specific questions regarding functionality or statements about the survey or quality of demos were omitted.

57% of respondents rated Print Management as Good.
57% of respondents E-Resource Management as Good.
71% of respondents rated Discovery as Good.
71% of respondents rated Patron Management as Good.
86% of respondents rated Staff Task Management as Good.
57% of respondents rated Metadata Management as Good.
57% of respondents rated Acquisitions Management as Good.
43% of respondents rated Reporting as Excellent.
43% of respondents rated Customer Support as Excellent.

Comments

"I remember more about this session but not necessarily specifics of the questions above (yes, having the list would have been helpful). I did like that the system was web-based, yet it still seemed to meet the same needs as the others."

"Out of the three options, I preferred Omega ILS. I'm of course bias as my own main concern is what can this do for the archives. It seemed this program offered a clear avenue for searching archive collections only, as well as offered flexibility for MARC cataloging of archives collections, which require a completely different set of fields than books. I think this system could be customized to increase efficiency in this regard (if I am remembering correctly). I think it reminded me more of the Gamma ILS, which I like."

"Liked Omega ILS a lot, especially the interface with regard to Circ procedures."

"I may be grading Omega ILS too harshly—I'm sure it really ranks good to excellent on all fronts. It's the most viable solution for SU at this time."

Appendix B

IMPLEMENTATION PLAN

Scope

Project is slated to start in July 2017 and be completed by January 2018. Project will consist of:

1. Migration of bibliographic and use data,
2. General configuration of system, including patron types, locations, and policy rules,
3. Training of staff by Omega ILS Company,
4. Configuring patron upload,
5. Configuring authentication,
6. Configuring State Share Catalog integration, and
7. Testing service internally and externally before going live.

Once migration is complete, we plan to bring the new system in production before the start of the Spring 2018 Term, with a tentative date of January 8.

Justification

With the system currently in place not serving the modern academic library needs and the cost outweighing the benefits, moving to a cheaper, web-based ILS will better serve our community and better serve SU Library's financial bottom line.

Goals and Objectives

   Successful migration of Omega ILS
   Improved user experience and library usage
   Budget savings for library

Risks

   Timely coordination between Library and IT
   Timely coordination between Procurement/Purchasing, the library, and Omega ILS Company
   Timely coordination between Library and Neighborhood Libraries Online for State Share Catalog configuration
   Staff not participating in training
   Staff resistant to change
   Quality of data we move into Omega ILS

Constraints

Budget and Scope are well-defined and should not be constraints. Time is the biggest constraint. Original timeline was much tighter, but coordination of cleaning up records and migration of data in a timely fashion will be key.

Project Team and Resources

Systems Librarian, Project Manager
Omega ILS Company Implementation & Training Team
Various members of library staff, specifically:
- Manager, Circulation
- Librarian, Acq & Collection Dev.
- Librarian, Tech Services
- Library Assistant, Technical Services
- Librarian, Access Services

Budget

The quote we have for implementation, training, and annual subscription is $52,800 for the first year. After that, for the next five years, the Hosting and Support Annual Subscription will be $21,500. This is significant savings compared to our current setup with far more benefits.

Cost-Benefit Analysis

Table 10.1. Alpha ILS Costs

Year	License and Support	NCIP	Local Hosting Cost Estimate by Campus IT	Total Cost
2017–2018	$46523.00	$5,000.00	$1,720.00	$53,243.00
2018–2019	$48,849.15	$5,250.00	$1,720.00	$55,819.15
2020–2021	$51,175.30	$5,512.50	$1,720.00	$58,407.80
2021–2022	$53,501.45	$5,788.13	$1,720.00	$61,009.58
2022–2023	$55,827.60	$6,077.53	$1,720.00	$63,625.13
2023–2024	$58,153.75	$6,381.41	$1,720.00	$66,255.16
Total	$314,030.25	$34,009.56	$10,320.00	$358,359.81

Table 10.2. Omega ILS Costs

Year	Hosting and Support	Implementation	Training	Total
2017–2018	$21,500.00	$27,700.00	$3,600.00	$52,800.00
2018–2019	$21,500.00			$21,500.00
2020–2021	$21,500.00			$21,500.00
2021–2022	$21,500.00			$21,500.00
2022–2023	$21,500.00			$21,500.00
2023–2024	$21,500.00			$21,500.00
Total	$129,000.00	$27,700.00	$3,600.00	$160,300.00

Table 10.3 Annual Cost Savings

Year	Annual Savings
2017–2018	$443.00
2018–2019	$34,319.15
2020–2021	$36,907.80
2021–2022	$39,509.58
2022–2023	$42,125.13
2023–2024	$44,755.16
Total	$198,059.81

Tentative Migration Timeline

The Project will begin in July 2017 and end January 2018.

July—Kick-off meeting
August—Data upload and review
September 25—All data uploaded and reviewed
October—Mapping of data, configuration, and setup of Patron Upload, Auth, and State Share Catalog integration
November—Test server up, circulation rules reviewed, and student life office contacted for marketing work
December—OPAC customization, Training, and Testing
January 2—Pre-Go Live Prep
January 8—Last data dump from Alpha ILS to Omega ILS
January 11—Go live

Table 10.4 Tentative Migration Timeline

Major Milestones	July	Aug	Sep	Oct	Nov	Dec	Jan 8
1. Kick-off meeting with Library Staff and Omega ILS Company	■						
2. Begin migration with initial data dump to Omega ILS Company		■					
3. Omega ILS Company setting up instance			■				
4. Configure and customize				■			
5. Training on site conducted by Omega ILS Company						■	
6. Migrate over rest of data							■
7. Go live							■

Stakeholders
SU Library Librarians & Staff
SU IT Networking & Systems
SU Community (All faculty, staff, and students)

Communication

Specific communication to SU Library stakeholders and SU community regarding Omega ILS migration steps and tasks will be done by the Systems Librarian and Library Director via the normal library channels.

Engaging SU Student Life to create student-centric marketing materials for an integrated marketing plan will be done in November.

Training of staff and developing some training resources and communications for our user community will be the most important part of our communications plan.

Closing Plan (Assessment and Lessons Learned)

A seamless cutover to Omega ILS with no interruptions for the SU community while realizing cost savings on systems expenses will be the ideal outcome. Higher use of library resources for AY 17-18 and overall higher user satisfaction both for SU library staff and SU community are two possible examples of assessment work that may be done.

Assessment and continued management of service should be done by all librarians and staff in their areas of expertise and in a collaborative effort. The creation of a library committee to formalize this ongoing need should be considered post-migration.

Index

Page references for figures are italicized.

Alma, 18, *28*, 45–46, 49–50, 98, 116
Amazon, 6, 50, 61, 79
Apache Group, 11
Archival Management Systems, 121
Archon, 122
Archivists' Toolkit, 123
ArchivesSpace, 124
Aspen Discovery, 81–83
AtoM, 125
Avram, Henriette, 28
Axmark, David, 11

Bell Labs, 7, 9
Berkeley Software Distribution (BSD), 3, 8–9
Blacklight, 83–86
Block, Carson, 16, 110
Bouis, Sonia, 31
Breeding, Marshall, 18–19, 29–30
Bywater Solutions, 34, 45, 48, 81–83, 112–13, 116

Carr, Les, 61
CERN, 42–43
cloud computing, 6, 11–12, 15, 24, 26n16, 61, 65, 72, 98, 123, 125–28, 133, 135, 143, 144, 146.
See also Software as a Service (SaaS)
commoditization, 18, 25, 27, 29, 30
Computer Systems Research Group (CSRG), 9
CORAL, 111–114
Counting Online Usage of Networked Electronic Resources (COUNTER) 110–11
COVID-19, 134

Devinim Software, 36
Digital Asset Management System (DAMS), 55–56
Digital Library Federation (DLF), 110
discovery systems, 77–93
Discovery Systems Era, 16–18
Drupal, 5, 63–65
DSpace, 58–61

EBSCO, 34, 44–46, 48–51, 78, 80, 89, 112–13, 115–18
Electronic Resources Management Initiative (ERMI), 110–111, 118–119
Electronic Resources Management Systems (ERMS), 109–10
Encoded Archival Description (EAD), 121–22

End User Era, 16
enterprise resource planning (ERP), 27, 29, 144
EPrints, 61–63
Equinox, 34, 38, 40, 99–101
Evergreen, *28*, 36–41
Ex Libris, 18, 28, 45, 80, 98–99, 102, 104

Fedora, 57, 63, 64, 66, 68, 71, 72n6
Ferraro, Joshua, 33,35
FOLIO, 43–49, 114–17
free software, 2, 4;
  and libre vs. gratis, 2
Free Software Foundation, 2, 4
freeware, 2, 19
FulfILLment, 99–101
Functional Requirements for Bibliographic Records (FRBR), 82, 88
Functionality Era, 16

Globalization of Information Resources Era, 16–17
GNU, 4, 8, 10–11, 14n31, 62
Google, 1, 6, 50, 79
Gueguen, Grechen, 67

hacker, 13n17
hacker ethic, 7–8
Harnad, Stevan, 61
Hatcher, Erik, 80, 85
Hedges, Stephen, 33
Horrowhenua Library Trust (HLT), 30, 32
Hyrax, *See* Samvera

IndexData, 46, 49, 51, 102–4, 117, 134
indexing software:
  Apache Solr, 59, 64, 79–89, 93, 103;
  Elasticsearch, 33–34, 42, 87, 125;
  Zebra, 33, 35, 46
Institutional Repository (IR), 55–56
Integrated Library System (ILS), 17–19, 23, 27–51.

See also Library Service Platform (LSP)
Interlibrary Loan (ILL), *See* Resource Sharing
Invenio, 41–43
Islandora, 63–66

Jewell, Timothy, 110

Kapito Communications, 30, 32, 35
Katz, Demian, 89–90
Knowledge Innovation Era, 16, 24
Kochtanek, Thomas, 16
Koha, *28*, 30–36

Lahmann, Andre, 90
LAMP, 11, 19, 25n10, 32, 62, 70, 79, 81, 87, 89, 111, 115, 123, 125, 127
Leonard, Troy, 37
Levy, Michael, 85
LibLime, 33–35
library automation, history of, 16–18
Library of Congress, 28, 78, 121
Library Services Platform (LSP), 18, 42–46, 49–50, 109–10, 113–14, 118, 134, 144–45.
See also Integrated Library System (ILS)

MAchine-Readable Cataloging (MARC), 28–29, 32–34, 59, 78, 85–86, 91, 122, 147
Marmot Library Network, 80–81, 87–88
Matthews, Joseph, 16, 24, 110
Microsoft, 1, 6, 9
multi-tenant, 18, 41, 43, 46–47, 67, 69, 115, 144–46

Nagy, Andrew, 80, 89
Nelsonville Public Library (NPL), 33, 35
NISO Circulation Interchange Protocol (NCIP), 33, 98–100, 103, 149
Noble, Mark, 81–83
North Carolina State University, 79, 128–29

Nowviskie, Bethany, 80, 85

OCLC, 57, 78, 80, 97–98, 102–3, 105
Omeka, 70–71
ONIX for Publications Licenses
    (ONIX-PL), 111, 119
Online Public Access Catalog (OPAC),
    17, 28, 34, 78–80, 84, 87, 93,
    118, 150
open access, xviii, 15, 24, 58, 128
Open Archives Initiative Protocol for
    Metadata Harvesting (OAI-PMH),
    59, 62, 64
Open Journal Systems (OJS), 127
Open Library Foundation (OLF), 15,
    47–48, 101–4, 114
Open Source Initiative (OSI), 2–3
open source software licenses:
    Apache 2.0, 5, 30, 47, 83, 101, 104;
    BSD, 5;
    description of, 3–4;
    GPL, General Public License, 2, 4–5,
    30, 38, 42, 47, 59, 62, 64, 81, 87, 89,
    99;
    MIT, 5, 30, 42;
    MPL, Mozilla Public License, 5
OpenURL, 18, 98, 110
operating system, 5, 7–11, 14n31, 19,
    25n11, 38, 46, 127, 143;
    BSD, 8–9;
    Linux, 5, 8–12, 19;
    Minix, 10;
    Multics, 7;
    Unix, 7–10

Pace, Andrew, 29
Parker, Ralph Halstead, 27–28
Pennsylvania Academic Library
    Consortium, Inc. (PALCI), 66–67,
    102–4
Pika, 87–89
Piščanc, Jordan, 58
Poulain, Paul, 34–35
Project ReShare, 101–4

ProQuest, 28, 45, 46, 50, 78, 80, 98, 104
Public Information Network for
    Electronic Services (PINES), 37–38

resource sharing, 97–105
Ritchie, Dennis, 7–8

Sadler, Elizabeth, 83, 85
Samvera, 66–69
SirsiDynix, 28, 49, 113–14
Software as a Service (SaaS), 12, 24,
    26n16, 36, 60, 65, 69, 71, 117, 143
Stallman, Richard, 4, 8, 13, 20
Standard Interchange Protocol version
    2.0 (SIP2), 33
Standardized Usage Statistics Harvesting
    Initiative (SUSHI), 110–11
SubJectsPlus, 126
Suma, 128
Systems Era, 16

Tanenbaum, Andrew, 10
Thompson, Ken, 7–8
TIND, 41–43, 50
Torvalds, Linus, 10, 25

vendor lock-in, 18, 25, 29–30, 33, 36,
    69, 117, 126, 134
VuFind, 89–93

Ward, Keely, 112
Web 2.0, 79–81, 86, 91, 94
Weber, Steven, 3–4, 7
Wenander, Marie, 44
Widenius, Monty, 11
Widigson, Marie, 44
WordPress, 5, 127
WorldShare Management Services
    (WMS), 18, 46, 50, 110, 116

YAZ, 46

Z39.50, 32, 98–100, 103
Zend, 129

About the Authors

Robert Wilson is systems librarian and assistant professor at Middle Tennessee State University's James E. Walker Library. He has been supporting, administering, and implementing open and closed source library systems since 2011 in school, public, and, most recently, academic libraries. He has also served in support analyst, technical lead, and implementation manager roles at a global library service provider. He has an MS in Information Systems from Middle Tennessee State University and an MSLIS from Drexel University.

James Mitchell is systems librarian at the University of North Alabama's Collier Library. Since 2012, James has been responsible for implementing technology solutions within archives and libraries in both public and academic libraries. He holds an MLIS from the University of Alabama.

www.ingramcontent.com/pod-product-compliance
Lightning Source LLC
Chambersburg PA
CBHW031711230426
43668CB00006B/180